COST OF CONFLICT
IN THE MIDDLE EAST

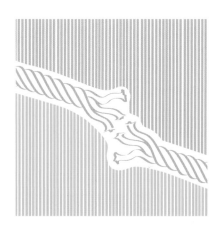

In cooperation with

AK Party, Turkey

Federal Department of Foreign Affairs, Switzerland

Ministry of Foreign Affairs, Norway

Qatar Foundation, Qatar

Strategic Foresight Group

C-306 Montana, Lokhandwala Complex, Andheri West, Mumbai 400053, India
E-mail: publications@strategicforesight.com

Authors : Sundeep Waslekar, Ilmas Futehally

Core Group : Egemen Bagis (Turkey), Thomas Greminger (Switzerland), Vidar Helgesen (Norway), Salman Shaikh (Qatar), Hesham Youssef (Arab League)

Additional Research Advice : Yair Hirschfeld (Israel), Jean-Daniel Ruch (Switzerland)

Principal Researcher : Gitanjali Bakshi

Creative Head : Preeti Rathi Motwani

SFG Research Team : Rohit Honawar, Devika Mistry, Sahiba Trivedi, Ambika Vishwanath

Research Input : Talaat Abdel Malek (Egypt), Hussein El Kamel (Egypt), Azza El Kholy (Egypt), Roger Edde (Lebanon), Esra Gurkaynak (Turkey), Aly Maher (Egypt), Eliane Metni (Lebanon), Saif Al Murikhi (Qatar), Ica Wahbeh (Jordan)

Research Support : Mahdi Abdel Hadi (Palestinian Territories), Riad Al Khouri (Lebanon), Sahar Al Qawasmi (Palestinian Territories), Mahmoud Labadi (Palestinian Territories), Mark Taylor (FAFO - Norway)

Production support : Media Logistics, Processed by Excel Computer Design Centre, Printed at Lifon Industries, Mumbai

Preface

The objective of this report is to provide comprehensive estimates of costs of conflict and potential benefits of peace in the Middle East. In doing so, we have focussed on people of the region and not merely matters that concern states. This report is essentially about human security in the Middle East.

It is necessary to clarify what we mean by 'conflict in the Middle East'. In the first few decades after Israel's birth in 1948, the term 'conflict' essentially referred to wars and antagonistic relationship between Israel and Arab countries in its neighbourhood. Once Israel signed peace treaties with Egypt and Jordan and entered into negotiations with the Palestine Liberation Organisation, the conflict seemed to be narrowing in its scope. A decade ago, the primary actors in the conflict involved Israel and PLO. There was also the unresolved conflict between Israel and Syria and internal strife in Lebanon, which had regional implications.

Since 2000, the conflict has metamorphosed into several conflicts. The Palestinians are now represented by Hamas and Fatah, two organisations that are at loggerheads with each other, though at times they negotiate truce under the auspices of Arab countries. Since 2003, the US invasion of Iraq has added another dimension. In 2006, the exchange of missiles between Israel and the Lebanon-based Hezbollah further complicated the conflict. It is widely believed that Iran supports Hamas and Hezbollah and thus is present in the Arab-Israeli conflict through proxies. In addition, the President of Iran has publicly threatened to wipe out Israel from the map and the United States has admonished Iran for its development of nuclear weapons, amidst speculation about a possible US or Israeli attack on Iran's nuclear sites. Al Qaeda and its affiliated terrorist network have pronounced a war against 'Jews and Crusaders'. Though Al Qaeda had its origins in the developments in Afghanistan and Pakistan, its rhetoric, manpower and support base is very much about the Middle East. Thus, what was an identity and territorial conflict in one geography a decade ago has now expanded into a multi-dimensional, cultural and psychological warfare of global dimensions. If we look ahead, there is a risk of this conflict getting even more complicated. A resurgent Russia may want to assert its interests in the region. China has developed several economic relationships. If history is any guide, extensive economic engagement often leads to political and security repercussions. In this report, we have focussed on the Arab-Israeli conflict but also reflected on the growing complexity of the situation.

It is necessary to explain what we mean by 'costs'. In this context our emphasis on human security is very important. States are concerned about measurable costs such as those having a bearing on resource allocation, arms race, destruction of assets, among others. People are concerned about costs that have a bearing on their living conditions, such as security at cafes and dignity at check-posts, opportunities for education, damage to environment and social fabric. Some costs have monetary value. It would be insensitive and inappropriate to interpret some other costs in financial terms. For instance, it is possible and useful to measure the economic burden of refugees for both home and host countries. However, it would be inappropriate to measure the economic costs of death of children. It would be useful to measure financial implications of farms and trees destroyed as they provide livelihood for farmers. However, it would be inappropriate to try to measure loss of biodiversity in terms of money. Life, of human beings and others in the ecosystem, is valuable in itself and not for the economic returns it may generate. Our report throws light on all such costs.

We have placed certain emphasis on opportunity costs. When people are involved in a conflict, their losses are not confined to what they have lost as compared to what they have. Their losses also include what they do not have that they could have had in the absence of conflict. In terms of opportunities for growth, economist Paul Collier has observed in his study of conflicts in Africa that a violent conflict reduces GDP growth rate by 2%. In the Strategic Foresight Group study on Cost of Conflict between India-Pakistan we had estimated 1% reduction in GDP growth rate for India. Our assessment was questioned by Indian economists who suggested that the losses would be closer to 2%. In the case of countries in the Middle East, the opportunity loss would be at least 2% reduction in GDP growth rate. Since, several countries in the Middle East have shown an ability to grow at 6%, we assume that a framework of peace and cooperation along with good governance and sound economic policies would enable the countries in the region to have a GDP growth rate of 8% per annum. Our report obviously goes beyond GDP to examine complexity and depth of issues in their various dimensions.

We have used 1991 as the benchmark year for most of our calculations. We believe that the Madrid Conference provided a historic opportunity to reverse history in the Middle East. It did not deliver hope since the conference was a one-time event. Had there been a semi-permanent conference, the outcome might have been different. Peace was possible then and it is possible in the next couple of years. Therefore, we have made some estimates using 1991 as the basis and another set of calculations using 2010 as the basis.

This report does not advocate any particular formula to resolve conflicts in the region. It is for the stakeholders to design the solution they can live with and indeed determine what future they want. We have presented four scenarios for 2025, if alternative courses of action are followed.

The fact that this report was supported by the leaders or governments of four neutral countries – Norway, Switzerland, Turkey and Qatar – and made possible by the intellectual participation of more than 50 distinguished experts from the Middle East speaks for their concern for truth. The election of a new President of the United States, as well new leaders in the region, provides a window of opportunity in 2009. It is not only for people of the Middle East but also for leaders of the international community to decide if they want to put an end to costs and accrue the peace dividend. We hope that this report will prove to be a useful instrument for the choices they make.

Sundeep Waslekar

January 2009

President, Strategic Foresight Group

Introduction

The research project "Cost of Conflict in the Middle East" is an innovative approach to engage the broad public, experts and leaders of the Middle East to reflect on how much they have lost because of the conflicts, and how much more they could lose in the future. Or, to put it positively, how much everybody could win should peace eventually happen.

The study undertaken by the Strategic Foresight Group is based on research tools that were developed for studies on the India-Pakistan and Sri Lanka conflicts. It also focuses on future costs, using scenario building methodology for the years 2009-2025. The study is based on extensive macro-level research, inputs from top Middle East experts, numerous discussions with persons from the region, and advice provided by international policy experts. As an analytical tool, this report assesses past, present and future costs in the region taking into consideration a wide range of parameters. Thereby, our understanding of the conflict patterns is dramatically broadened, and so is our perception of the options that can be used to foster conflict prevention and resolution.

Conflicts in the Middle East have persisted for at least sixty years. Despite numerous initiatives, plans, road maps and processes on all tracks by governments and non-governmental actors, the ultimate goal – a just and lasting peace – remains illusive. As the Israeli-Palestinian conflict lies at the heart of the whole region's dynamics, its resolution would have huge positive effects throughout the Middle East. The Madrid Conference and the Oslo Process marked the beginning of a decade, the nineties, providing hope that a solution was at hand at last. Yet promises have not materialised - neither the Camp David talks, nor the Arab peace initiative, nor the Annapolis conference have so far resulted in tangible success. The lack of political will or courage, the power of extremist forces, or simply the complexity of the issues can be blamed for this. Meanwhile violence or the risk of violence remains a daily nightmare for everyone.

Therefore, new initiatives and particularly new broader approaches are welcome. One of them could be the cost of conflict approach. The cost of conflict methodology takes into account different costs a conflict generates, including economic, military, environmental, social and political costs. It differentiates between costs to the people and to the states engaged in a conflict as well as to the international community. It contrasts these costs with the benefits that may derive from peace. The approach considers direct costs of conflict (for instance, human deaths, military expenditure, economic losses and the destruction of physical infrastructure) as well as indirect costs that measure the impact of conflict on a society (for instance, costs of migration, humiliation, growth of extremism, and lack of civil society).

Two main conclusions can be drawn from the report. Firstly, the enormity and diversity of the direct costs caused by the continued existence of conflicts, wars and instability in the Middle East is hampering the smooth development of each and every society in the region. Secondly, the magnitude of the gains that peace could bring to the whole region and beyond is presented in striking charts and figures. These data, magnificently documented, show that the understandable feelings of fear and injustice that are at the root of the conflict are in urgent need of being overcome.

The Middle East has always been a strategically important region where many outside players (such as the USA, the European Union or Russia) are involved. Considering the enormity of the costs evidenced in this report, which have direct or indirect negative consequences for the whole world, the necessity of an international intervention is inescapable. Indeed, it is in the best interest of all countries in the world to see the conflicts in the Middle East being solved. The facts in this report should prompt all concerned international actors to intensify their efforts for a lasting solution on an urgent basis. They would certainly wish to take their own share of the dividends of peace.

This report should sensitise different audiences all over the Middle East and the wider world. Experts, opinion leaders and decision makers will find many concrete, precise arguments in the report to promote peace-oriented policies. The public at large in the Middle East will also easily realize that, beyond speeches and rhetoric, peace would bring tangible results in their own life. Last but not least, this report is aimed at the young generation, for it is they who will most suffer or benefit from the decisions their elders will take now and in the years to come.

Ambassador Thomas Greminger
Federal Department of Foreign Affairs, Switzerland

Contents

Chapter 1 : Economic Costs

INTRODUCTION

The economic costs refer to several different kinds of costs.
- Direct costs incurred due to destruction and damage caused by war
- Opportunity costs reflecting growth that did not take place due to conflict environment
- Opportunity costs reflecting regional trade and investment opportunities missed
- Indirect costs

The countries in the Middle East, with a few exceptions, have sound fundamentals for growth in terms of high quality human resources, physical infrastructure, reasonably open economies, urbanised population and international exposure. They don't face the problems encountered by a number of developing countries in Asia, Africa and Latin America where over dependence on agriculture, structural bottlenecks, and infrastructure problems render fast growth difficult. The failure to achieve a higher growth in the Middle East is to a large extent the function of political uncertainties and the image of the region as one associated with extremism and violent conflicts.

This is also a rather exceptional part of the world not to have any comprehensive regional free trade area agreement unlike Europe, North America, South Asia, South East Asia, Latin America and Africa. The Gulf Cooperation Council is limited in its scope. The Greater Arab Free Trade Agreement is not much effective. Israel only trades with the Palestinian Territories, Jordan, Egypt and Qatar – in the entire Middle East. There is no economic grouping that can bring together Israel, Saudi Arabia, Iran, Syria, Lebanon and others for preferential and cooperative trade and economic cooperation.

Besides the opportunity costs of missed opportunities, equally important are the direct costs on account of destruction caused by wars or armed hostilities of some kind.

Cost of Conflict in the Middle East

GDP Growth Rate: 1990s and 2000-2008 (%)

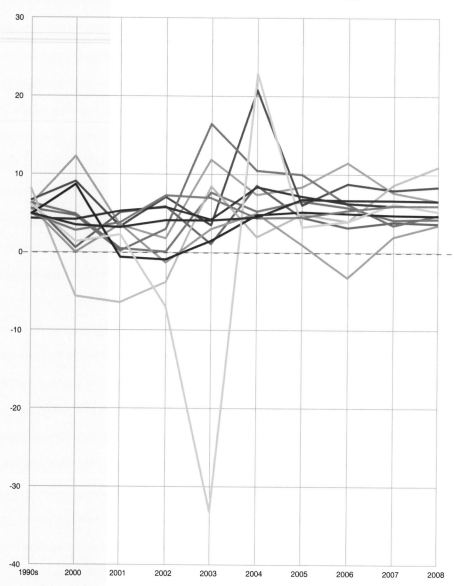

| Egypt | Iran | Iraq | Israel | Jordan | Kuwait | Lebanon | OPT | Qatar | Saudi Arabia | Syria | UAE |

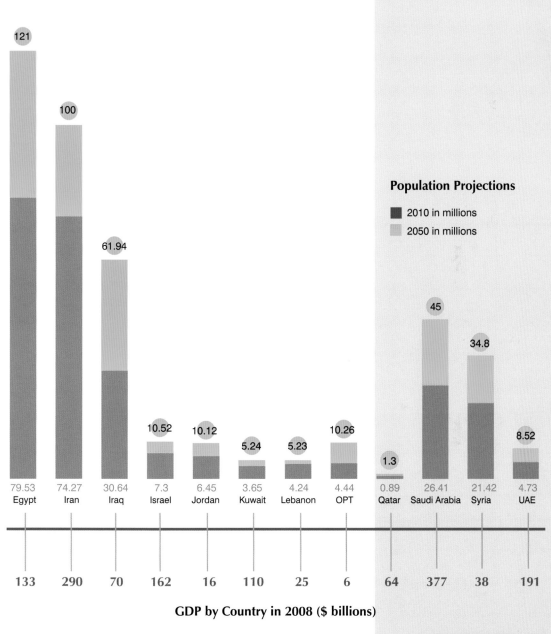

Population Projections

- 2010 in millions
- 2050 in millions

121	100	61.94	10.52	10.12	5.24	5.23	10.26	1.3	45	34.8	8.52
79.53	74.27	30.64	7.3	6.45	3.65	4.24	4.44	0.89	26.41	21.42	4.73
Egypt	Iran	Iraq	Israel	Jordan	Kuwait	Lebanon	OPT	Qatar	Saudi Arabia	Syria	UAE
133	290	70	162	16	110	25	6	64	377	38	191

GDP by Country in 2008 ($ billions)

Cost of Conflict in the Middle East

$12,000,00

0,000,000

twelve trillion

The Madrid and Oslo processes provided an outstanding opportunity for peace and cooperation in the Middle East. They were instrumental in breaking the deadlock between the Israeli and Palestinian people. Had the leaders demonstrated vision in capturing the Madrid Opportunity to enter into a comprehensive peace and cooperation agreement across the region, the region would be experiencing different kinds of economic performance than the current ones. The peace intervals have demonstrated that countries can grow at 6% GDP per annum. In the 1990s the Palestinian Territories grew at 8% per annum. It should have been possible for all countries to grow at the average rate of at least 8% per annum in the last two decades. The failure to do so has resulted in this opportunity cost for the period 1991-2010 (in 2006 US dollar values).

OPPORTUNITY COST OF CONFLICT
(In 2006 $ billion)

GDP (Projected) 2010
GDP (Peace) 2010

| | 143 | 241 |
Egypt

| | 306 | 570 |
Iran

| | 59 | 297 |
Iraq

| | 18 | 29 |
Jordan

| | 24 | 48 |
Lebanon

| | 122 | 189 |
Kuwait

| | 170 | 323 |
Israel

| | 5 | 11 |
OPT

| | 36 | 63 |
Syria

| | 77.3 | 81.9 |
Qatar

| | 442 | 1009 |
Saudi Arabia

| | 267 | 325 |
UAE

Technical Notes

1. GDP Growth Rates 1991-2006: actual.

2. GDP Growth Rates 2007-2010: projected on the basis of hypothesis as given below, based on average rates of the two years, 2006, 2007.

Egypt	6.70%
Iran	6.00%
Iraq	4.00%
Israel	5.00%
Jordan	6.70%
Kuwait	4.85%
Lebanon	2.00%
OPT	6.60%
Qatar	8.4%
Saudi Arabia	5.00%
Syria	3.50%
UAE	10.00%

3. GDP (Peace) 2006 = [342.59 x actual GDP 2006] ÷ UN Stats index number for 2006 (with 1990 base).

4. GDP (Peace) Growth Rates pegged at 8 % p.a. for 1991-2010 for all countries

5. It is assumed that oil exporting countries would have been able to diversify their economies in the absence of conflict in the region by attracting investments, technologies and trading centres. Thus, much of their growth would emanate from economic modernisation, despite somewhat lowering of oil prices.

6. Calculations made on the basis of GDP figures for 2006, as provided in UN stats.

Cost of Conflict in the Middle East

2. OPPORTUNITY COST RELATIVE TO SIZE OF ECONOMIES

The opportunity cost for 1991-2010 appears largest for Saudi Arabia at $4.5 trillion or one third of the total opportunity loss incurred by 13 countries in the region. However, as compared to the size of its economy, Iraq has suffered the largest loss. Its GDP could have been more than 30 times of its present size. Moreover, we have used 1990 as the base year. Iraq had already spent a decade in a war with Iran by that time. If we examine Iraq's opportunity loss since 1980 when it entered a period of warfare – first with Iran, then Kuwait and finally the West – it would be at least 50 times of its GDP in 2010.

Opportunity Cost in Comparison with the Size of Economies
(In 2006 $ billions)

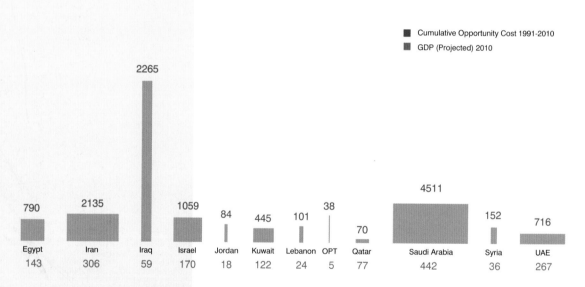

3. EVERYBODY'S LOSS

The opportunity loss of $12 trillion for 1991-2010 means every citizen has lost. An average Israeli, Saudi, Palestinian and Lebanese would have enjoyed double the income level whereas an average Iraqi would have been 4 times richer.

Per Capita Losses in 2010 (in 2006 Constant Dollars)

● GDP (Projected) 2010
● GDP (Peace) 2010

Egypt 1789 | 3022

Iran 4142 | 7728

Iraq 2375 | 9681

Israel 23304 | 44241

Jordan 2781 | 4490

Lebanon 5618 | 11205

Kuwait 17837 | 27615

OPT 1220 | 2427

Qatar 86854 | 92022

Saudi Arabia 16645 | 37969

Syria 1664 | 2896

UAE 54698 | 66492

Cost of Conflict in the Middle East

4. WAR, CIVIL WAR & GROWTH

The inverse relationship between war and economic growth is obvious. During Iran-Iraq War of the 1980s, both countries witnessed decline in their income year after year. Similarly, Iraq saw drop in its GDP during the two Gulf Wars. Israel, Lebanon and Palestine territories have had the same experience. When there was no war or civil war, these economies could grow by more than 6% GDP growth rate per annum. Israel does have an arms industry. However, its positive impact on economic growth appears marginal, since it accounts for only 3.5% of GDP.

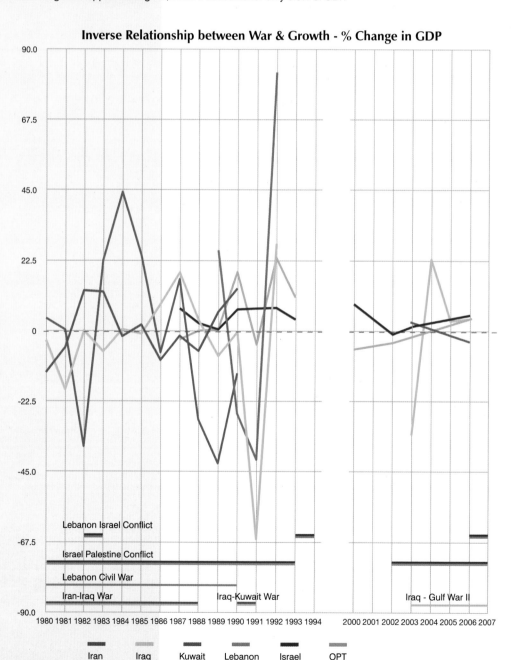

Inverse Relationship between War & Growth - % Change in GDP

5. COST OF IRAQ WAR

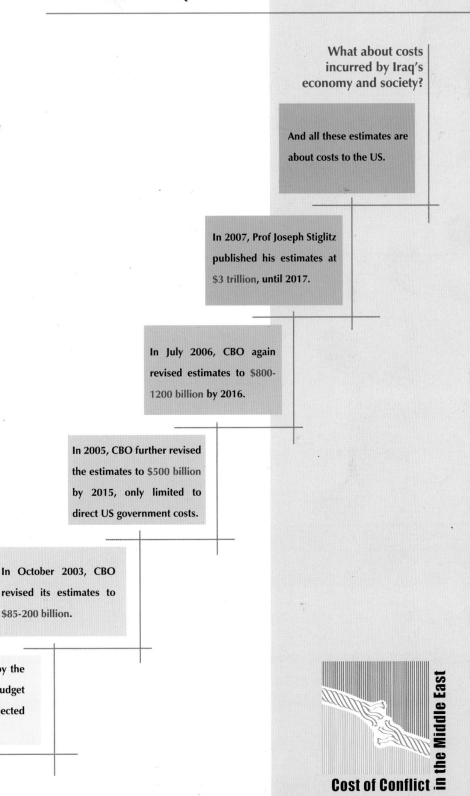

What about costs incurred by Iraq's economy and society?

And all these estimates are about costs to the US.

In 2007, Prof Joseph Stiglitz published his estimates at $3 trillion, until 2017.

In July 2006, CBO again revised estimates to $800-1200 billion by 2016.

In 2005, CBO further revised the estimates to $500 billion by 2015, only limited to direct US government costs.

In October 2003, CBO revised its estimates to $85-200 billion.

In 2002, a study by the Congressional Budget Office (CBO) projected $50-60 billion.

Cost of Conflict in the Middle East

6. REFUGEES & BRAIN DRAIN

Between March 2003 and September 2008, a period of five and half years, about 5 million Iraqis became refugees or internally displaced persons. The flight of Iraqis has become the largest forced displacement in the history of the Middle East – exceeding the Palestinian exodus of 1948. Among the Iraqi refugees and internally displaced persons about 4 million are women and children and 1 million wage-earners.

Loss of income opportunity, if the wage-earners are compared to...

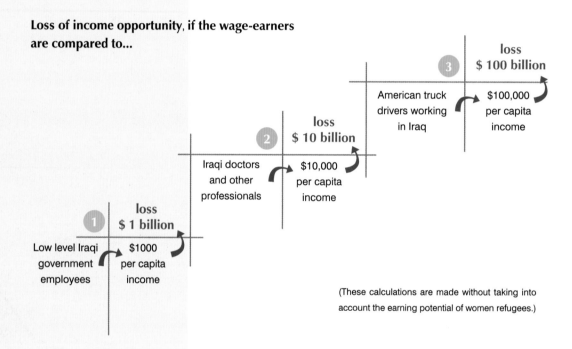

loss
$ 100 billion

3

American truck
drivers working
in Iraq

$100,000
per capita
income

loss
$ 10 billion

2

Iraqi doctors
and other
professionals

$10,000
per capita
income

loss
$ 1 billion

1

Low level Iraqi
government
employees

$1000
per capita
income

(These calculations are made without taking into account the earning potential of women refugees.)

The Middle East has become a land of refugees. Besides 5 million Iraqi refugees and IDPs, there are about 4.5 million Palestinian refugees and IDPs.

Iran loses more than 150,000 educated persons every year in the form of the flight of intellectual capital. If an average Iranian professional is able to contribute to gross capital formation of $40,000 per year or 10 times of per capital GDP, Iran is losing $6 billion a year in growth opportunities.

7. TRAVAILS OF HOST COUNTRIES

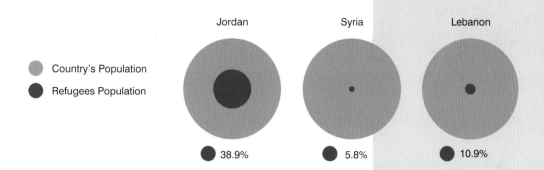

○ Country's Population

● Refugees Population

Jordan   Syria   Lebanon

● 38.9%   ● 5.8%   ● 10.9%

Jordan is accommodating refugees to the extent of more than a third of its population. In comparison, can the United States accommodate more than 100 million refugees in its population of 300 million? Jordan spends almost 7% of its GDP on refugees. In comparison, can the United States afford an expenditure of $ one trillion on refugees?

Jordan, Syria, Iraq and the Palestinian territories pay a cost that cannot be reflected in official expenditure	• Pressure on land and housing prices • Inflation in food and fuel prices • Criminalisation of society • Growth of prostitution • Pressure on social services, especially education and healthcare

The Result is Hostility from Hosts towards the Refugees

- Iraq's neighbours are imposing highly restrictive passport and visa requirements.
- Saudi Arabia is building a $7 billion high tech barrier on its border.
- Jordan is restricting the entry of Iraqi men ages 18 to 35.
- Jordan is issuing a new G series passport that is tamper proof and difficult to obtain in Iraq.
- In the Iraqi Kurdish areas or the predominately Shia areas, IDPs are barred entry, denied access to civil services and not allowed to stay for a long time. It is estimated that 47% of IDPs do not have access to the Public Distribution System.
- Another group to be targeted is the Iraqi Christians; some 150,000 Assyrians are recorded to live in Jordan to escape extortion, killing, forced taxation, and church bombings in Iraq.

Jordan, Syria, Kuwait, Lebanon and Saudi Arabia are non signatories to the 1951 Refugee Convention. Lebanon is a non signatory to the 1967 Protocol on the Status of Refugees.

Cost of Conflict in the Middle East

Crude Oil Production in Selected Oil Exporting Countries in the Middle East

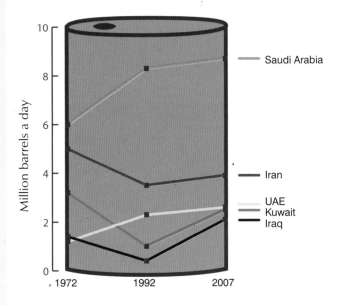

In the absence of war, Iraq could produce an extra 2 million bpd and Iran 1 million bpd in 2008.

Loss per year @ $50 per barrel of oil.

Iran $18 billion = 4% of GDP

Iraq $36.5 billion = 80% of GDP

These calculations are made on the basis of the lowest price seen in 2008, by the time this report went to press.

9. ISRAEL HEZBOLLAH CONFLICT IN 2006

Costs for Northern Israel

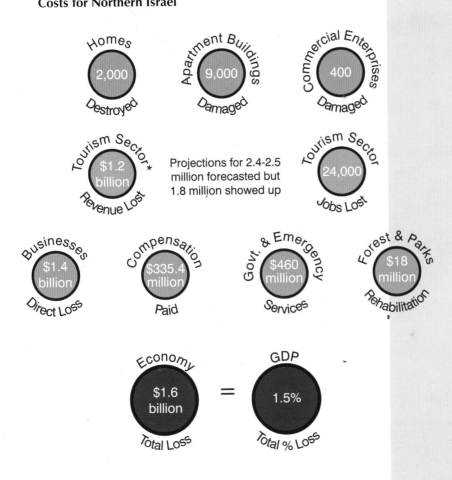

Homes
2,000
Destroyed

Apartment Buildings
9,000
Damaged

Commercial Enterprises
400
Damaged

Tourism Sector*
$1.2 billion
Revenue Lost

Projections for 2.4-2.5 million forecasted but 1.8 million showed up

Tourism Sector
24,000
Jobs Lost

Businesses
$1.4 billion
Direct Loss

Compensation
$335.4 million
Paid

Govt. & Emergency
$460 million
Services

Forest & Parks
$18 million
Rehabilitation

Economy
$1.6 billion
Total Loss

=

GDP
1.5%
Total % Loss

*Tourism Ministry estimates that for every 100,000 tourists, $200 million are earned and 4,000 jobs are created.

The damage in Israel was mostly restricted to the Northern part of Israel, where small businesses were especially hard hit. This is significant in light of the fact that 20% of Israel's population resides there. Nationally, the sector hit the hardest was the tourism sector.

Cost of Conflict in the Middle East

Costs for Lebanon

Transportation Total Damage $470 million = Roads, Bridges Est. Damage $415 million + Airports Est. Damage $55 million

Public & Private Utilities Total $419 million = Electricity Est. Damage $226 million + Communications Est. Damage $116 million + Communications Est. Damage $77 million

Industrial Facilities $215 million 30% bombed   Military Institutions $16 million   Fuel Distribution $15 million Stations

Housing & Commercial Space $2406 million   Health & Education $34 million 60% of hospitals ceased to function

Tourism Revenue Loss $3-4 billion   No. of Tourists Forecasted 1.6 million   Tourism Fall 5-6%

FDI / VC

$3 billion

on hold or cancelled

Loss of Output

$2.2 billion

Airport

$170 million

Losses

Port

$65 million

Losses

Oil Spill

$175 million

Est. Cleanup

Forest Fires

$4.6 million

Estimated

Indirect Economic

$250 million

Estimated

Hezbollah RRR

$300 million

Estimated

Govt. Spending

Rebuilding

$318 million

Estimated

Homes Rebuilding

$181 million

Estimated

Infrastructure Repair

$454 million

Estimated

Civilians Displaced

$52 million

Estimated

Economy Loss

$3.6 billion

Total Estimated

=

GDP

8%

Total Loss

Cost of Conflict in the Middle East

10. BOYCOTT CONTINUES

Israel, Iran and several of the Arab States are missing out on significant trade opportunities due to lack of trade between Israel and her neighbours until the 1990s, and very marginal trade with only a few of them since 1994.

Israel's trade in the region:

Egypt	✓
Iran	✗
Iraq	✗
Jordan	✓
Kuwait	✗
Lebanon	✗
Occupied Palestinian Territories	✓
Qatar	✓
Saudi Arabia	✗
Syria	✗
UAE	✗

The Arab Boycott of Israeli goods has evolved since 1948. It is at three levels; one, primary boycott prohibited Arab people and the states from doing any business with Israel. Second, the secondary boycott attempts to prevent business anywhere in the world from any economic activity with Israel threatening them with economic retaliation in return (against international law). Thirdly, a tertiary boycott that punishes firms that deals with blacklisted businesses. The last one even applies to international shipping, aviation and tourism - e.g. most ships and airplanes calling on Israel are barred from Arab ports, airplanes en route to and from Israel cannot even fly over Arab countries and Israeli or any travellers with Israeli visas in their passports may not enter most Arab countries. Though some Arab countries agreed to lift the boycott in the mid-1990s, there is in practice very little trade between Israel and Arab countries.

According to the estimates of the Israeli Chamber of Commerce, Israel loses 10% of its export potential due to the Arab boycott. Thus, in the current decade from 2001-2010, Israel lost an export opportunity of $30-50 billion (in 2006 US dollars). The Arab states also lost an opportunity to export $10 billion to Israel during the same period, assuming that they could provide 5% of Israel's import needs in a friendly atmosphere. In addition, the Arab States and Iran miss out on the possibilities of importing Israeli goods and technologies.

Israel spends about $10-15 billion per year importing oil as per the market prices prevailing in 2008. The Gulf States and Iran could export most of it, which would be possible in the absence of conflict – as was the case of oil trade between Israel and Iran during the Shah years. Considering the current state of conflict, the Gulf States and Iran together would lose at least $30 billion during 2008-2010 due to the opportunity cost of not exporting oil to Israel.

The lack of trade between Israel and the Arab States, as well as Iran is abnormal. Most countries in the world involved in conflicts engage in trade – such as the robust trade and investments between People's Republic of China and Taiwan and growing trade between India and Pakistan or Turkey and Greece.

Cost of Conflict in the Middle East

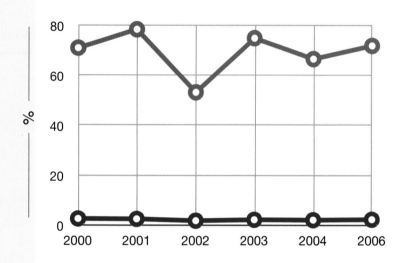

○ Total PA trade with Israel / Total Israeli trade

● PA trade with Israel / Total PA trade

Palestinian Trade with Arab countries in the last decade accounted for less than 10% of total Palestinian Trade. It is projected that access to GCC markets can increase Palestinian exports to these markets by over 50%.

Chapter 2 : Military Costs

INTRODUCTION

The countries in the Middle East are involved in conflicts and arms race at various levels.

- Conflicts between Arab countries and Israel
- Conflicts between Arab countries and external powers
- Hostility between Israel and Iran
- Rivalry between Arab countries and Iran
- Internal conflicts

These conflicts occur at various levels of intensity

- Acts of terror
- Low intensity warfare
- Civil war
- Attacks by states without a full scale war
- Troops mobilisation without a full scale war
- Wars

Military costs include costs incurred in all kinds of warfare including the preparedness for a war. They include human lives lost including military personnel, armed groups and civilians as well as financial costs.

The Middle East has emerged as the most militarised region in the world by all parameters

- the proportion of GDP provided for defence expenditure;
- the number of young men committed to the security sector in the form of regulars, reserves, and para-military groups;
- civilian casualties.

Cost of Conflict in the Middle East

HUMAN COSTS OF MAJOR WARS IN THE MIDDLE EAST, 1948-2007

COUNTRY	Arab-Israeli War 1948-49	Arab-Israeli War 1956-57 (Suez war)	Arab Israeli War 1967 (The Six day + Israeli Egyptian war)	Arab Israeli War 1973 (Yom Kippur War)	Lebanon Israel 1975-90 (Lebanese Civil War)	Lebanon Israel 1978 (Operation Litani)	Lebanon Israel 1982 (Operation Peace for Galilee)
Egypt	2,000	2-4,000	15-20,000	5-15,000			
Israel	3-6,000	189-231	1-1,700	2.5-3,000		20	1,216
Iran							
Iraq	500			125-200			
Jordan	1,000		6,000				
Kuwait							
Lebanon	500				115,000	1,168	17,825
Palestine	3,000				37,000	2-300	
Saudi Arabia							
Syria	1,000		1-2,500	3-8,000			
USA					260		
UK	23	22					
Other		10			58		
TOTAL BY CONFLICT	11,023-14,023	2,221-4,263	23,000-30,200	10,625-26,200	152,318-162,318	1,388-1,488	19,041

N.B. : Discrepancy in tally due to differences in total number killed and break-up by country.
Numbers include both civilian and military deaths.

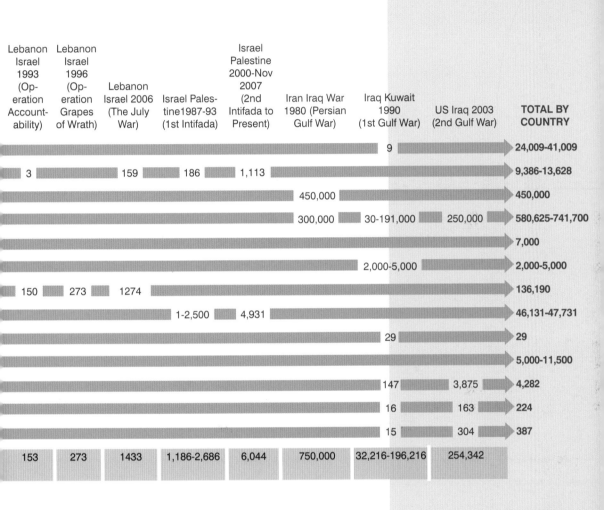

Lebanon Israel 1993 (Operation Accountability)	Lebanon Israel 1996 (Operation Grapes of Wrath)	Lebanon Israel 2006 (The July War)	Israel Palestine 1987-93 (1st Intifada)	Israel Palestine 2000-Nov 2007 (2nd Intifada to Present)	Iran Iraq War 1980 (Persian Gulf War)	Iraq Kuwait 1990 (1st Gulf War)	US Iraq 2003 (2nd Gulf War)	TOTAL BY COUNTRY
						9		24,009-41,009
3		159	186	1,113				9,386-13,628
					450,000			450,000
					300,000	30-191,000	250,000	580,625-741,700
								7,000
						2,000-5,000		2,000-5,000
150	273	1274						136,190
			1-2,500	4,931				46,131-47,731
						29		29
								5,000-11,500
						147	3,875	4,282
						16	163	224
						15	304	387
153	273	1433	1,186-2,686	6,044	750,000	32,216-196,216	254,342	

Cost of Conflict in the Middle East

NUCLEAR NON-PROLIFERATION TREATY
& COMPREHENSIVE TEST BAN TREATY

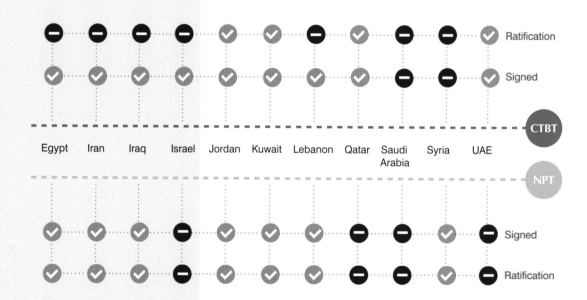

| | Egypt | Iran | Iraq | Israel | Jordan | Kuwait | Lebanon | Qatar | Saudi Arabia | Syria | UAE | |

1. HUMAN COSTS OF MAJOR WARS

It is difficult to have reliable estimates of casualties in any war. The Middle East earns bad press around the world for the conflict between Israel and the Palestinian people, extended to a broader conflict between Israel and the Arab states and people. However, in terms of human costs, other conflicts inflict heavier damage.

Consider this:

The three Arab-Israeli Wars (1948-49, 1967, 1973) together cost somewhere between 40,000 and 80,000 lives. Israel's wars with Lebanon or groups within Lebanon (1978, 1982, 1993, 1996, and 2006) resulted in more than 20,000 human deaths. The two Intifada phases (1987-93 and 2000 onwards) have cost 10,000 lives. Thus, together the human loss is somewhere between 70,000 and 110,000.

Iraq-Iran War (1980s) resulted in a toll somewhere between 500,000 and 1,000,000. The First Gulf War toll was somewhere between 100,000 and 200,000. The Second Gulf War, including internal strife in Iraq, has so far resulted in a toll of somewhere between 100,000 and 500,000 depending on the source.

Therefore, the conflict in the Middle East cannot be seen from the narrow prism of the Israel-Palestinian conflict. There are other fault-lines in the region, which make the conflict multi-dimensional.

Direct losses of human lives in the two Intifada phases were around 10,000. The losses from the two Gulf Wars together could be around half a million or 50 times as much.

While the world's attention is focussed on Israel's conflict with the Arabs - particularly the Palestinians - much greater damage is done by the US war in Iraq and radical-moderate conflict involving Iran.

Cost of Conflict in the Middle East

2. MILITARY EXPENDITURE

The SIPRI yearbook 2007 has published data on the military expenditure in most countries in the world from 1997 to 2005.

The Middle East has the highest military expenditure burden in the world. Between 1997 and 2005, the Middle East had an average of 6% of their GDP allocated to military spending while the world average for military expenditure stood at 2% of GDP in 2005. Further, the global data is heavily lop-sided because of the United States military expenditure.

Out of the world's 10 largest military spenders as a proportion of GDP, 7 are from the Middle East.

Top 10

Others ■
Middle East ▦

World's Highest Military Expenditure as % of GDP, 2004 and 2005

COUNTRY	2004	2005
Afghanistan	11.9	9.9
Burundi	6.6	6.2
Eritrea	23.0 +	23.0 +
Israel	8.3	9.7
Iran	4.5	5.8
Iraq	I	I
Oman	12.0	11.9
Saudi Arabia	8.4	8.2
Syria	6.4	5.1
Yemen	5.7	7.0

+ Eritrea: figures for 2004 and 2005 not available. Trends from 1998 indicate higher than 23%.

I = impossible to measure but huge by all circumstantial indicators

Total Military Expenditure by Country

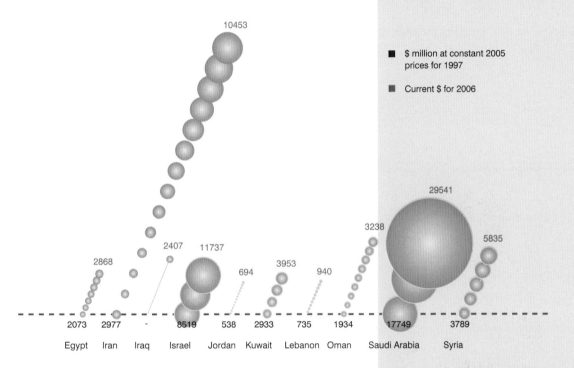

Legend:
- ■ $ million at constant 2005 prices for 1997
- ■ Current $ for 2006

	Egypt	Iran	Iraq	Israel	Jordan	Kuwait	Lebanon	Oman	Saudi Arabia	Syria
Top values	2868	2407		11737 10453	694	3953	940	3238	29541	5835
Bottom values	2073	2977	-	8519	538	2933	735	1934	17749	3789

There is a race going on in the Middle East – an arms race. Saudi Arabia leaps in a decade from $18 billion to $30 billion, Iran from $3 billion to $10 billion, Israel from $8 billion to $12 billion – and this was in the times before the dollar began its slide. As a region, it registered the highest increase in the world in the decade ending 2006, closely followed by the United States, which is extensively involved in the Middle East in any case.

Cost of Conflict in the Middle East

Health and Military Expenditure as % of GDP in 2004

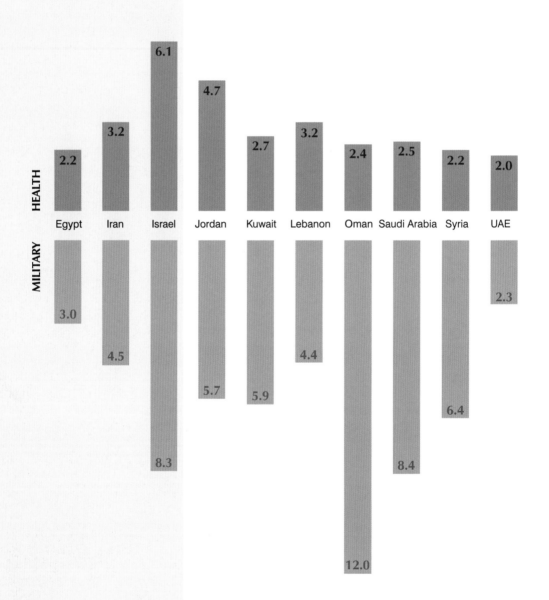

4. BOTTOMLESS PIT

The US announced $63 billion military assistance and arms sales package for Israel, Egypt, and the Gulf States in 2007, over the next 10 years.	Israel	$30 billion
	Egypt	$13 billion
	Gulf States(*)	$20 billion

(*) Saudi Arabia, UAE, Kuwait, Qatar, Bahrain, Oman

At one stroke, military expenditure of these states increases by 10% every year through the next decade. Also, it provokes Iran and Syria at least to match with extra additional expenditure. Thus, the cumulative spending on military in the region will be double in the next decade of 2007-2016 as compared to the previous period of 10 years.

Cumulative Military Expenditure in 2005 dollars

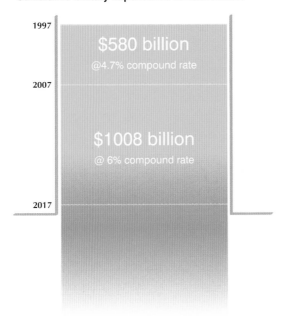

1997

$580 billion
@4.7% compound rate

2007

$1008 billion
@ 6% compound rate

2017

2027

The expected expenditure on defence in the next decade for the Middle East is almost equal to the entire GDP of Israel, Egypt, Saudi Arabia, Kuwait, Qatar, Bahrain and Syria, or more than half of the GDP of the entire region from Iran to Egypt in 2008, or almost comparable to the entire world's annual military expenditure in the same year.

If there is a significant outbreak of war in the next decade, the expenditure can be expected to increase even to higher levels.

Will the security of people of the Middle East increase by spending a trillion dollars equivalent on arms in the next decade?

Cost of Conflict in the Middle East

5. MILITARIZATION OF THE SOCIETY

Armed Forces by Country : Military personnel per million people

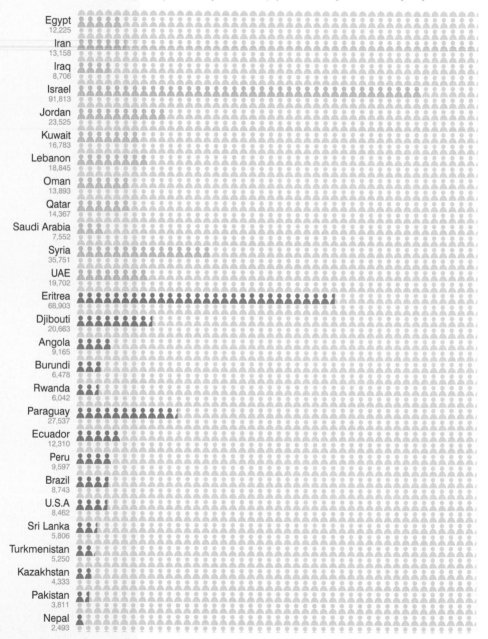

Country	
Egypt	12,225
Iran	13,158
Iraq	8,706
Israel	91,813
Jordan	23,525
Kuwait	16,783
Lebanon	18,845
Oman	13,893
Qatar	14,367
Saudi Arabia	7,552
Syria	35,751
UAE	19,702
Eritrea	68,903
Djibouti	20,663
Angola	9,165
Burundi	6,478
Rwanda	6,042
Paraguay	27,537
Ecuador	12,310
Peru	9,597
Brazil	8,743
U.S.A	8,462
Sri Lanka	5,806
Turkmenistan	5,250
Kazakhstan	4,333
Pakistan	3,811
Nepal	2,493

The Middle East is by far the most militarized region in the world in terms of per capita military personnel. Certain countries like Israel, Syria, Lebanon and Iran have a compulsory conscription service.

The Middle East competes with Eritrea, Djibouti and Paraguay in the militarization of its people. Not too far from the Middle East, Sri Lanka is the most militarized society in South Asia. And the degree of Sri Lanka's militarization is 1/15th that of Israel.

6. BEYOND REGULARS AND RESERVES

Number of Paramilitary Forces by Country
(per million people)

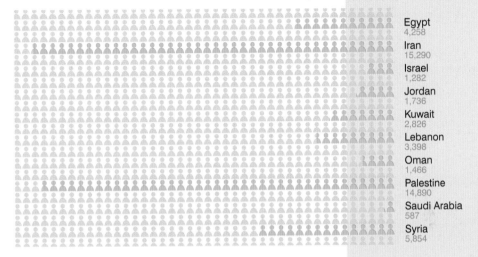

Egypt
4,258

Iran
15,290

Israel
1,282

Jordan
1,736

Kuwait
2,826

Lebanon
3,398

Oman
1,466

Palestine
14,890

Saudi Arabia
587

Syria
5,854

Estimated Strength of Insurgency in Iraq: 2004-2007

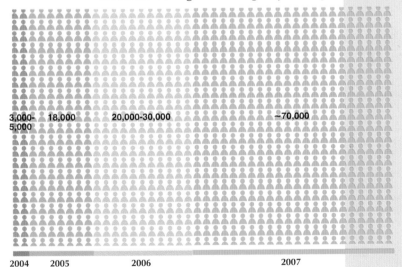

3,000-5,000   18,000   20,000-30,000   ~70,000

2004   2005   2006   2007

According to reports, a number of men from Shia militia units such as the Badr organization and the Mehdi army as well as from the Sunni Awakening Council have infiltrated into Iraqi security forces. This poses a potentially dangerous dynamic within the Iraqi security apparatus as there are now both Shia militia forces and Sunni tribesmen, thirsting for a stake in the Iraqi power game.

Cost of Conflict in the Middle East

If military personnel, reserves, para-military and foreign troops are all included, the Middle East has more than 5-6 million armed people. The United States with a population almost the same as the Middle East (around 300 million) has 2.5 million armed forces, including army, navy, air force, marines and reserves. India with more than 3 times the population of the Middle East has 2.5 million forces, equally divided between the military and para-military. The human resources in the Middle East are diverted to the security sector in a much greater proportion than any other part of the world. Accordingly, the security sector has a vested interest to continue conflict - subtly or directly encouraged by agents of the arms industry.

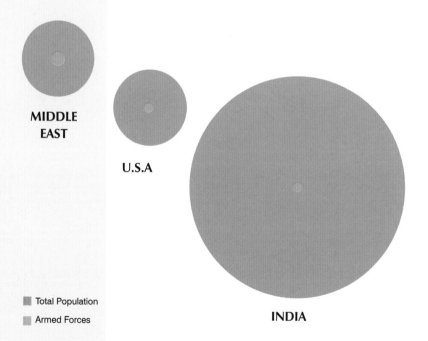

MIDDLE EAST

U.S.A

INDIA

■ Total Population
■ Armed Forces

7. US MILITARY PERSONNEL

The US currently has more than 222,000 military personnel stationed in the Middle East, a number that is greater than the military manpower of 8 out of 14 countries in the region.

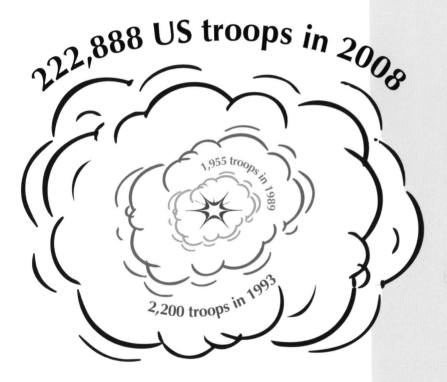

222,888 US troops in 2008

1,955 troops in 1989

2,200 troops in 1993

The US military presence in the region has increased 120 times in the last 20 years. It has increased 100 times in the last 15 years, since 1993 - much of it since 2003 due to the war in Iraq.

Cost of Conflict in the Middle East

8. NUCLEAR ACTIVITY

NUCLEAR CAPACITY IN THE MIDDLE EAST

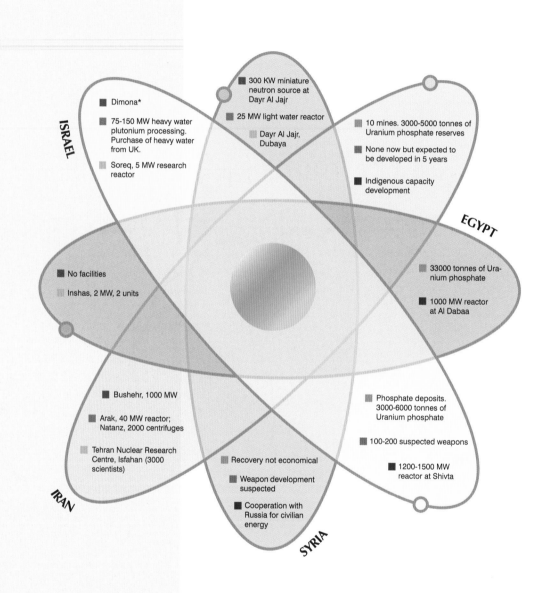

- Power Plant
- Heavy Water Production Plant and Enrichment Facilities
- Nuclear Research Centres/ Reactors
- Mines/Deposits
- Suspicion about Weapons
- Future Plans

*Israel keeps information about its nuclear sites a secret, but Prime Minister David Ben Gurion admitted to the existence of the Dimona plant in 1960. This plant is now considered to be at risk for accidents due to its age.

According to the World Nuclear Association, an industry group, 15 million cubic meters of seawater is desalinated every day in the Middle East, mostly in hydrocarbon-powered plants. Now the GCC states are looking to switch from hydro-carbon to nuclear energy for desalination and this is one of the biggest incentives for civil nuclear power in the Middle East. GCC has launched a study on the feasibility of nuclear power for desalination, while the United Arab Emirates signed an agreement for nuclear cooperation with France in January 2008. The problem is that the transition to nuclear weapons from civilian nuclear power projects cannot be easily detected.

Currently, civilian nuclear programmes and plans in the Arab countries are for peaceful purposes. However, there is a serious academic speculation that the development of nuclear weapons by Israel and Iran will one day motivate Saudi Arabia and Egypt to develop weapons. If this happens, Turkey will want to join the race. It is also possible that some of the Arab states may want to develop weapons in anticipation of developments in Iran. A race driven by expectations about the plans of rival states is possible just as a naval race between Britain and Germany had taken place at the beginning of the last century leading to the First World War.

Cost of Conflict in the Middle East

NUCLEAR CAPABLE MISSILES BY COUNTRY (range /payload)

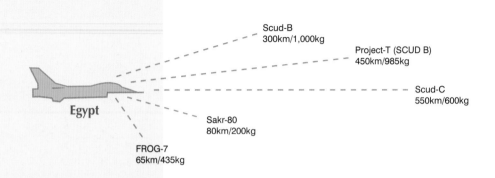

Scud-B
300km/1,000kg

Project-T (SCUD B)
450km/985kg

Scud-C
550km/600kg

Egypt

Sakr-80
80km/200kg

FROG-7
65km/435kg

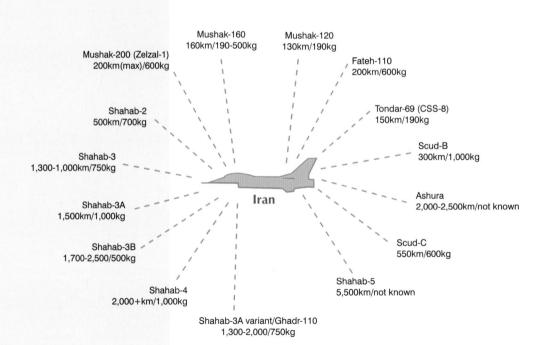

Mushak-160
160km/190-500kg

Mushak-120
130km/190kg

Mushak-200 (Zelzal-1)
200km(max)/600kg

Fateh-110
200km/600kg

Shahab-2
500km/700kg

Tondar-69 (CSS-8)
150km/190kg

Shahab-3
1,300-1,000km/750kg

Scud-B
300km/1,000kg

Iran

Shahab-3A
1,500km/1,000kg

Ashura
2,000-2,500km/not known

Shahab-3B
1,700-2,500/500kg

Scud-C
550km/600kg

Shahab-4
2,000+km/1,000kg

Shahab-5
5,500km/not known

Shahab-3A variant/Ghadr-110
1,300-2,000/750kg

Al Fatah
160km/200-300kg

Iraq

Al Samoud II
180-200km/300kg

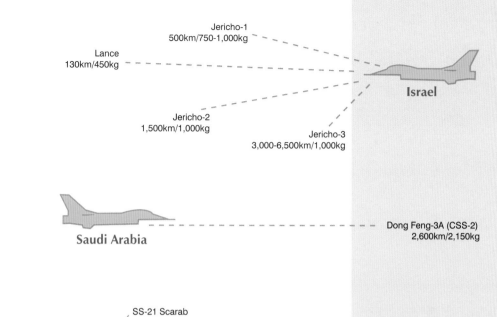

Jericho-1
500km/750-1,000kg

Lance
130km/450kg

Israel

Jericho-2
1,500km/1,000kg

Jericho-3
3,000-6,500km/1,000kg

Saudi Arabia

Dong Feng-3A (CSS-2)
2,600km/2,150kg

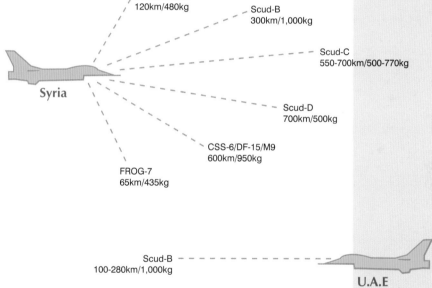

SS-21 Scarab
120km/480kg

Scud-B
300km/1,000kg

Scud-C
550-700km/500-770kg

Syria

Scud-D
700km/500kg

CSS-6/DF-15/M9
600km/950kg

FROG-7
65km/435kg

Scud-B
100-280km/1,000kg

U.A.E

Short-range ballistic missiles, travel less than 1,000 km;
Medium-range ballistic missiles, travel between 1,000-3,000 km;
Intermediate-range ballistic missiles, travel between 3,000-5,500 km;
Intercontinental ballistic missile (ICBMs), travel more than 5,500 km.

In July 2008, Iran test-fired 9 missiles, including at least one medium-range
ballistic missile, capable of reaching Israel.

Cost of Conflict in the Middle East

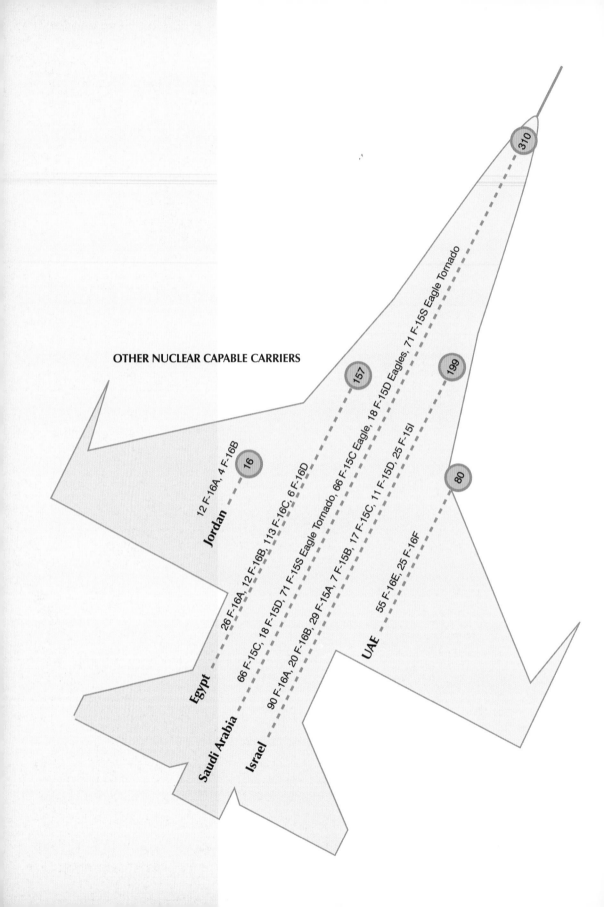

OTHER NUCLEAR CAPABLE CARRIERS

Jordan — 16 — 12 F-16A, 4 F-16B

Egypt — 157 — 26 F-16A, 12 F-16B, 113 F-16C, 6 F-16D

Saudi Arabia — 66 F-15C, 18 F-15D, 71 F-15S Eagle Tornado

Israel — 199 — 90 F-16A, 20 F-16B, 29 F-15A, 7 F-15B, 17 F-15C, 11 F-15D, 25 F-15I

UAE — 80 — 55 F-16E, 25 F-16F

310 — 66 F-15C Eagle, 18 F-15D Eagles, 71 F-15S Eagle Tornado

10. NUCLEAR ARMAGEDDON: 2017

The countries in the Middle East have delivery systems for nuclear weapons. They are in the process of acquiring nuclear energy, which can be used for nuclear weapons. What is the worst that can happen? The scenario outlined below is for the purpose of illustrating consequences - it is not our assumption that it will play out.

The Setting

Date : circa 2017; 50th anniversary of the 1967 war.

Nuclear weapons : Israel more than 200 weapons, Iran 20 weapons, Saudi Arabia 4 or 5 weapons – all unaccounted, untested and unacknowledged by the respective countries.

Delivery systems: Israel – Jericho 3; Iran – Shahab 4; Saudi Arabia – Dong Feng; hundreds of F-16 Fighting Falcons all over the region.

International environment : International community fails to initiate a credible and sustainable process, acceptable to all parties in the region to address all conflicts and their inter-linkages in the region.

Regional environment : Excessive use of force by Israel against pockets of population in Lebanon and the Palestinian territory; violent attacks against Israeli civilian targets by various non-state groups practising terror methods; heated exchanges between Israel and Iran at a high frequency; Lack of united Arab leadership; failure in Iraq.

Social environment : extremely high frustration among youth and armed forces in the region

The Attack

Israel has committed to a No First Use Policy since the 1960s and honoured this commitment during the 1973 war and the First Gulf War, despite being hit by missiles. In this scenario, Israel launches a conventional attack on Iran's military installation. Iran launches a nuclear strike against Israel.

Iran uses a 15 kiloton weapon. The attack takes place at a height of 600 meters. Since Iran is not confident of target accuracy, it launches a triple attack on Tel Aviv area. While one missile fails to deliver payload, two hit the target within a kilometer of each other.

All people within 1.1 km of the hypocentre die instantly. People in the second zone in a radius of almost 2 km from the hypocentre suffer from mechanical

Cost of Conflict in the Middle East

The Range of Missiles in the Middle East

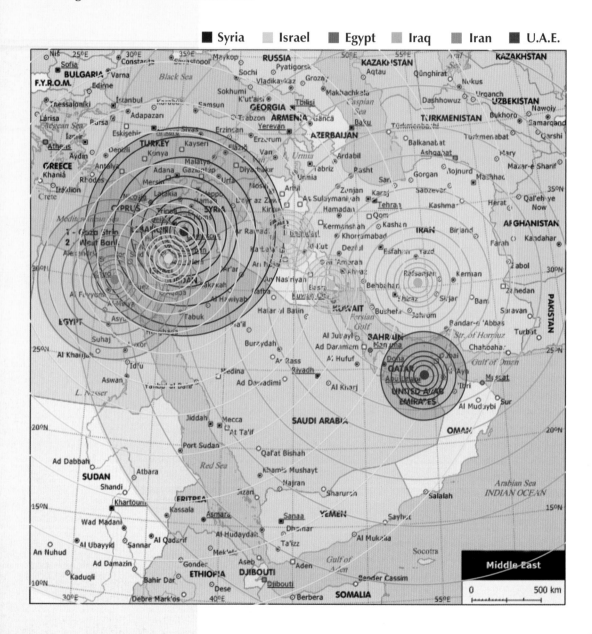

effect of a pressure blow, followed by blast overpressure and high velocity winds. Physical objects such as cars, poles, bridges are propelled outwards like missiles. While the initial death toll will be 50%, it will eventually increase to 90%. In the area beyond a radius of 2 km but within 3.5 km, there will be partial fires, small explosions and a complete breakdown of infrastructure.

In a swift retaliation, Israel uses a 50 kiloton weapon. The attack takes place at a height of 600 meters with clear visibility in early hours of the morning. It is a weekday. Children have just reported to the schools. Office goers are on their way. Israel attacks a few different cities simultaneously.

All the people within 2.5 km of the hypocentre of the attack will be killed. All buildings will be destroyed. All objects that can catch fire will burn out. The school children will be the biggest number of victims. In the second circle beyond a radius of 2.5 km but within 5 km, the immediate casualty rate will be 50%. However, it will go up to 70-80% in the subsequent weeks due to the death of those succumbing to burn and radiation injuries. In the third circle of a radius of 7 km, the immediate death toll will be 10% due to flying objects and collapse of weak buildings. It will increase to 50% in the subsequent weeks due to the injured succumbing to burn injuries.

Since Israel is confident of the accuracy of the attack, it attacks a few different cities with one bomb on each city focussed on a high commercial value or military targets.

In either case, it is important to note that the nuclear explosion results in the release of great amount of energy in the form of X-rays that get absorbed in the air, increasing the temperature of the area around hypocentre and creating a fireball. While it expands, the fireball cools down by emitting radiation. Within 0.1 milliseconds the radius of the fireball can be 15 meters for the smaller attack (Iranian attack) and temperature around 300,000 degree Celsius. Together, the hot air, the products of explosion and other debris rise to form a mushroom cloud. As a result of this effect, the entire area around the hypocentre (1.1 km of Tel Aviv and 2.5 km of Tehran) will be totally devastated with no survival and no chance of recovery of physical assets.

While the impact beyond the first circle around the hypocentre is less damaging in terms of physical destruction, the psychological impact, panic, breakdown of infrastructure, and the collapse of the social system is totally devastating.

The precise impact of an attack will vary according to two types of details – (1) time of the year, time of the day, weather conditions, winds, size of weapon and the altitude at which it explodes (2) population density, closeness of population to other targets, social-economic systems.

There is bound to be asymmetrical impact of two attacks in the short run, depending on the details mentioned above. However, in the medium run, both societies come out of the tragedy as extremely weak, vulnerable, and psychologically destroyed.

Cost of Conflict in the Middle East

Here we have used the smallest possible bombs as examples. In reality in 2017, both Israel and Iran will have an ability to deliver much higher payload.

Death Toll
About 50 million, comparable to the Second World War.

Consequences
A nuclear attack essentially robs the involved societies of their future. There is an impact on several fronts.

Health
- Inadequate medical facilities to provide specialised treatment to radiation victims;
- Acute survival syndrome including disorientation, fear, helplessness, nervous breakdown and apathy;
- Radiation effects including leukemia, cancer of intestine and reproductive organs, chromosomal damage, birth defects, vision defects, hair loss, etc.;
- Psychological setback to entire population.

Economy
- Total collapse of infrastructure including ports, road, trains, and telecommunication systems;
- Capital flight, disruption in trade, inflation, unemployment, imposition of trade and aid sanctions (except humanitarian aid);
- Collapse of public finance and taxation system;
- Destruction of records of financial and industrial institutions;
- If oil wells or gas reserves are near the hypocentre, oil spills and fires spreading over several miles and destroying all assets on the way.

Environment
- An area of 10 to 25 sq km will be unfit for inhabitation for a few generations.

Political
- Loss of sovereignty of all countries concerned;
- International isolation (unlike an earthquake or Tsunami which attracts worldwide sympathy, a nuclear exchange would invoke disdain);
- Extension of conflict from two players to several more players and the risk of use of nuclear, chemical and other weapons of mass destruction by them;
- Collapse of governments and regimes.

Global
- End of faith in core human values;
- Breakdown of international order;
- End of the world as we know it, either leading to a World War or reordering of global priorities.

Chapter 3 : Environmental Costs

INTRODUCTION

The Middle East has abundant oil resources and scarcity of water. Wars and violent conflicts can damage both these vital resources. The experience of the two Gulf Wars as well as the Israel-Hezbollah conflict in the summer of 2006 provides evidence of how environment can be a direct casualty of conflict. There is an adverse impact on health, bio-diversity and eco-systems of the region.

Economists measure the financial costs of environmental damage resulting from wars. Such exercises serve limited utility. Environmental protection should be considered as a value in itself. Health of the environment is essential for long-term survival of humanity in each part of the world.

The general phenomenon of global warming should be distinguished from the specific environmental costs of conflict. Expert studies show that deliberate and large-scale damage to natural resources in a war adds to global warming in a specific way. Conversely, the consequences of global warming, climate change and depletion of water can give rise to new conflicts. The inability to deal effectively with cross border environmental challenges is a significant indirect cost of conflict.

The conflicts in the Middle East from 1948 to 2008 were essentially political with strong social and religious dimensions. The damage to environment was a cost of these conflicts. However, in the future, environment – in particular water scarcity – may prove to be both cause and cost of conflict.

Cost of Conflict in the Middle East

Annual per Capita Renewable Fresh Water Availability in the Middle East

(in cubic meters)

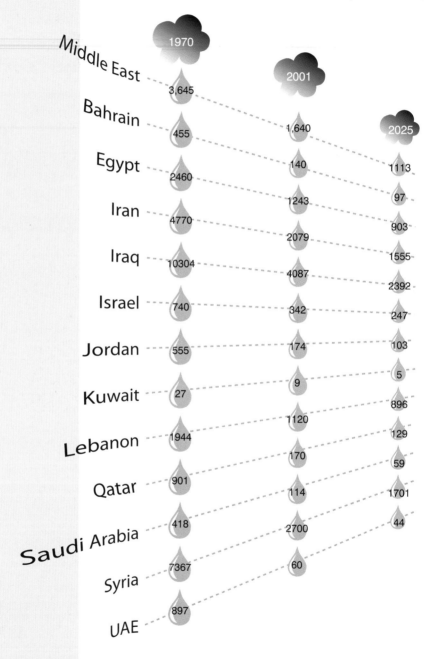

'Water-scarce' countries have an average of less than 1,000 cubic meters of renewable freshwater per person per year. A majority of the countries in the Middle East have already fallen considerably below this mark.

1. SPILLS, FLAMES & WELLS OF WARS

Environmental Consequences of Oil Related Damage

First Gulf War: 1990-1991

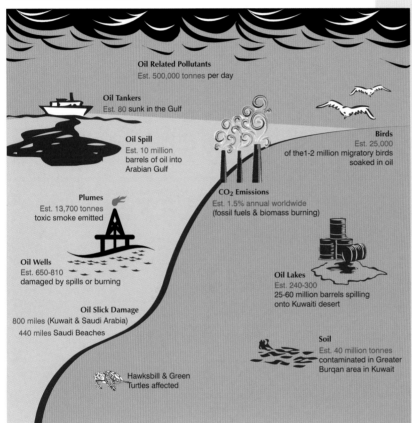

Human Costs

Kuwaitis killed
Est. 100+
from oil fumes

Gulf War Syndrome
Est. 100,000
US Veterans

According to Iraqi estimates, 15 million barrels of oil and 1.5 million cubic meters of petroleum products were burnt during the First Gulf War. It took 9 months to extinguish all Iraqi oil wells. On an average most beaches contaminated by oil slicks take 5 years to recover, whereas beaches affected during the First Gulf War needed more than a decade for recovery.

The war caused severe landscape degradation as well.

In Kuwait, an estimated 375,000 bunkers and trenches were hollowed into the ground. About 50% of the desert surface was compacted. 20% of tree cover in the country was felled as a result of the war.

In Iraq, 160 sq. km of forest land was destroyed and Iraqi marshlands shrunk from 15,000 sq. km to an astounding 50 sq. km, displacing a 100-300,000 people who lived in the area. Presently only 10% of people living in Iraqi marshlands can lead a traditional life of subsistence.

Cost of Conflict in the Middle East

Israel-Hezbollah War: 2006

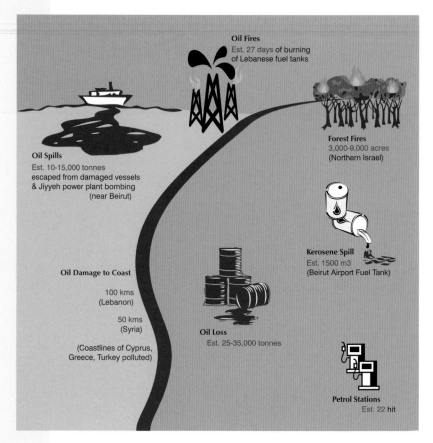

Oil Fires
Est. 27 days of burning
of Lebanese fuel tanks

Forest Fires
3,000-9,000 acres
(Northern Israel)

Oil Spills
Est. 10-15,000 tonnes
escaped from damaged vessels
& Jiyyeh power plant bombing
(near Beirut)

Kerosene Spill
Est. 1500 m3
(Beirut Airport Fuel Tank)

Oil Damage to Coast

100 kms
(Lebanon)

50 kms
(Syria)

(Coastlines of Cyprus,
Greece, Turkey polluted)

Oil Loss
Est. 25-35,000 tonnes

Petrol Stations
Est. 22 hit

The damage to critical infrastructure in Lebanon during the July 2006 war was extensive and severe. Statistics show that for every 1 tonne of oil spill to be cleaned up, 10 tonnes of hazardous material is created. In the case of oil spills, at best a mere 10-15% of oil is recovered.

During the First Gulf War, 10 million barrels of oil were spilt in the sea, while 45 million barrels were spilt in the Kuwaiti desert. In a future war, if the volume of oil spill only doubles to 100-120 million barrels a day, it would be equal to 1 day of oil supply for the whole world in the next decade.

2. DEPLETED URANIUM SHELLS

Depleted Uranium Shells Use by the United States (in tonnes)

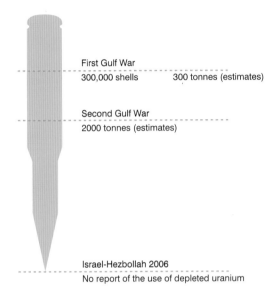

First Gulf War
300,000 shells   300 tonnes (estimates)

Second Gulf War
2000 tonnes (estimates)

Israel-Hezbollah 2006
No report of the use of depleted uranium

For comparison, the use of Deplete Uranium (DU) ammunition by the US was 9 tonnes and 3 tonnes respectively in Kosovo and Bosnia-Herzegovina. Clean up operations require soil removal and deactivation costing an estimated $4-5 billion for 200 hectares. Furthermore, DU ammunition is expected to contaminate the environment for 25-35 years. A secret US Military Study revealed that 50 tonnes of depleted uranium pollution inhaled could cause up to half a million additional cancer deaths over several decades.

Cost of Conflict in the Middle East

Environmental Consequences Of Water Related Damage

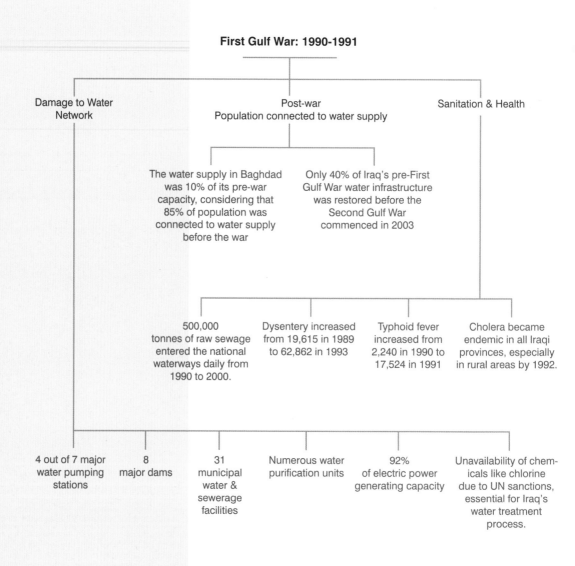

First Gulf War: 1990-1991

Damage to Water Network

Post-war
Population connected to water supply

Sanitation & Health

The water supply in Baghdad was 10% of its pre-war capacity, considering that 85% of population was connected to water supply before the war

Only 40% of Iraq's pre-First Gulf War water infrastructure was restored before the Second Gulf War commenced in 2003

500,000 tonnes of raw sewage entered the national waterways daily from 1990 to 2000.

Dysentery increased from 19,615 in 1989 to 62,862 in 1993

Typhoid fever increased from 2,240 in 1990 to 17,524 in 1991

Cholera became endemic in all Iraqi provinces, especially in rural areas by 1992.

4 out of 7 major water pumping stations

8 major dams

31 municipal water & sewerage facilities

Numerous water purification units

92% of electric power generating capacity

Unavailability of chemicals like chlorine due to UN sanctions, essential for Iraq's water treatment process.

The First Gulf War caused untold marine damage at the Iraqi port of Umm Qasr and the Khawr Al Zubayr as well as in the Shatt Al Arab waterways. About 80 ships were sunk during the conflict damaging marine life.

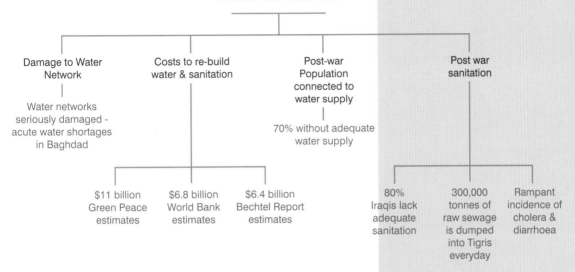

Second Gulf War: 2003

Damage to Water Network

Water networks seriously damaged - acute water shortages in Baghdad

Costs to re-build water & sanitation

$11 billion Green Peace estimates

$6.8 billion World Bank estimates

$6.4 billion Bechtel Report estimates

Post-war Population connected to water supply

70% without adequate water supply

Post war sanitation

80% Iraqis lack adequate sanitation

300,000 tonnes of raw sewage is dumped into Tigris everyday

Rampant incidence of cholera & diarrhoea

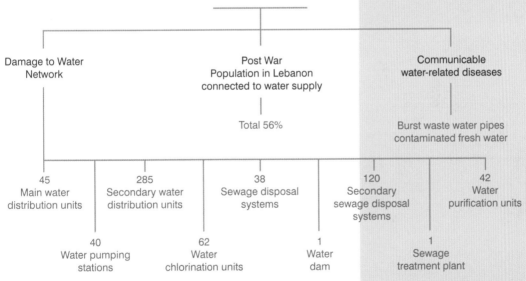

Israel-Hezbollah War: 2006

Damage to Water Network

Post War Population in Lebanon connected to water supply

Total 56%

Communicable water-related diseases

Burst waste water pipes contaminated fresh water

45
Main water distribution units

285
Secondary water distribution units

38
Sewage disposal systems

120
Secondary sewage disposal systems

42
Water purification units

40
Water pumping stations

62
Water chlorination units

1
Water dam

1
Sewage treatment plant

Streambeds, other water resources and agricultural fields were contaminated with UXOs (Unexploded Ordinances). It took more than a year to clear. Irrigation infrastructure along the Litani canal suffered severe damage. It will take several years to rebuild. South Lebanon experienced the worst damage where agriculture constitutes 70% of all household income.

Cost of Conflict in the Middle East

Water Dependency Ratio in the Middle East By Country

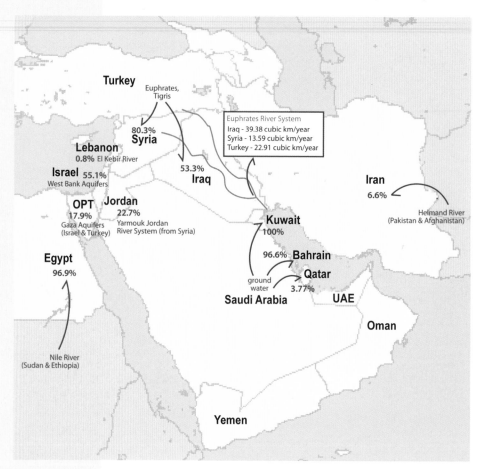

Dependency Ratio indicates the proportion of renewable fresh water resources that originate outside the country. Bahrain, Egypt, Iraq, Israel, Kuwait and Syria have a dependency ratio above 50% and hence are highly dependent on other countries for their freshwater resources.

Iraq and Syria depend on the Euphrates to a large extent for agriculture. Any future conflict that interrupts free flow of the river can severely undermine the life-system of farmers in Iraq.

The Jordan River is one of the most complex and contested water resources in the Middle East. Since the 4 tributaries originate in Syria, Golan Heights, Lebanon and Israel respectively, ownership becomes extremely complex.

Jordan River - 4 Tributaries

Yarmouk (Syria)
Banias (Golan Heights)
Hasbani (Lebanon)
Dan (Israel)

West Bank Coastal and Mountain Aquifers

West Bank Groundwater Allocation to Israel & Palestine (mcm/year)

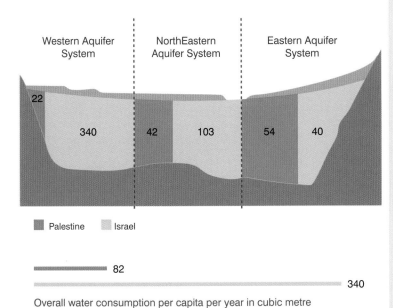

Safe pumping rate = 55 mcm/year
Current pumping rate = 120 mcm/year

Overall water consumption per capita per year in cubic metre

There are currently two main problems that Israel and Palestinian authorities face with regards to water:

a) The West Bank aquifers are technically under the territory of the Palestinian National Authority (PNA) but used by Israel, with Israel taking more than 80% of water. It pumps water from these aquifers through outlets based within Israeli territory and claims joint rights over the water.

b) Salt water intrusion in the Gaza coastal aquifers due to over pumping.

Cost of Conflict in the Middle East

Shatt Al Arab Waterway:

200 km in length ▬
Confluence of Tigris & Euphrates river systems

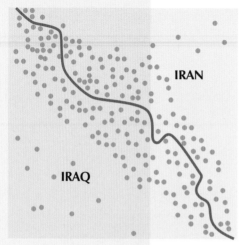

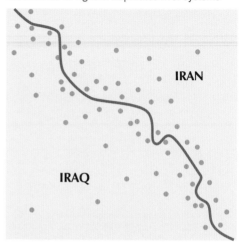

- Mid 1970s: 17-18 million a fifth of the world's 90 million palm trees

- By 2002 more than 14 million or 80% of the palm trees were wiped out, partly due to war

A border dispute over the waterway was one of the main reasons that led to the Iran-Iraq war in 1980s. Perhaps the group of people that suffered the most during the dispute were the marsh Arab tribes that lived on both sides of the waterway. The Shatt Al Arab waterway is Iraq's only outlet to the Persian Gulf and thus, it forms the country's only access to the sea.

The water systems in the Middle East are extremely inter-linked. In each war, water supplies and sanitation are damaged, reducing their efficacy for all countries concerned. The Israeli and Palestinian leaders and experts often express concern about the use of water as a weapon in a future conflict. Merely because water has not been a direct reason behind war in the past does not mean it will not be so in the future. Indeed, not only in the Middle East but also in other parts of the world, depleting water resources, may give rise to violent conflicts in the 21st century. Conflicts over water and water scarcity problem can be dealt with by finding practical solutions through dialogue and cooperation. An ongoing escalation of conflict over water may lead to the destruction of water installations and to a substantial worsening of water scarcity in the region.

Integrated Water Development

Water Co-operation

Egypt ══════════ 1959 Nile Waters Agreement ══════════ Sudan
Application of technology on the Nile River
to solve water problems

Iraq ══════════ 1975 Co-operation of the Tabqa Dam ══════════ Syria
Agreement to allocate equitable flow of Euphrates
to Syria (60%) and Iraq (40%)

Turkey ══════════ 1987 arrangement over the Attaturk Dam ══════════ Syria
Releasing 500 cubic meter/sec of Euphrates water to Syria
until the completion of the construction of Ataturk dam

Turkey ══════════ 1987 Peace Pipeline Project ══════════ Gulf Countries
Transfer of freshwater from Seyhan and Ceyhan to
countries in the Arabian peninsula. If enacted would be longest
international pipeline system - 6,550 km long, 6 million cubic meters a day

Co-generation of non-conventional water-resources

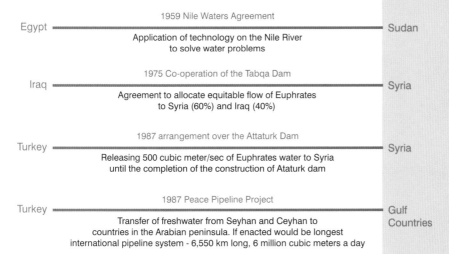

Palestine

Convey
seawater from
Mediterranean to
Dead Sea which could be
used in electricity generation,
cooling & solar power

Jordan   1980 Hydro-power scheme for   Israel
Mediterranean-Dead Sea Canal

Jordan   Peace Drainage Canal   Israel

Brackish water reclamation
scheme in the lower Jordan
river which would protect
water quality and
produce new fresh
potable water

Palestine

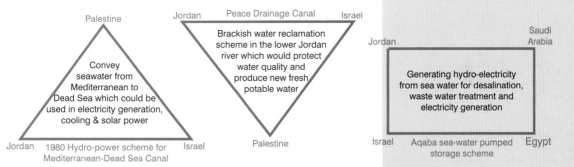

Jordan   Saudi Arabia

Generating hydro-electricity
from sea water for desalination,
waste water treatment and
electricity generation

Israel   Aqaba sea-water pumped   Egypt
storage scheme

Importation by pipeline, tankers, barges or floating water bags

Manavgat-Mediterranean Scheme

Turkey ══════════ Palestine
Using tugs and bags to transport
freshwater from Turkey to coastal
towns and cities in the Middle
East.

Israel

Diversions in a peaceful future

Nile to Gaza and Israel;
Euphrates from Iraq to North Jordan;
Shatt Al Arab from Iraq to Kuwait and Iran to Qatar

Cost of Conflict in the Middle East

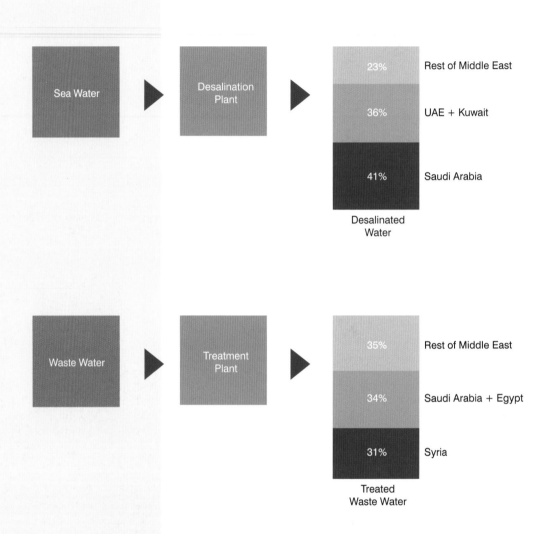

Saudi Arabia, Syria, UAE, Kuwait and Egypt are heavily dependent on treated or desalinated water. Hence, damage to these facilities during conflict can severely cut off the freshwater supply and create a crisis for clean water in these countries.

6. CARBON EMISSIONS IN A FUTURE WAR

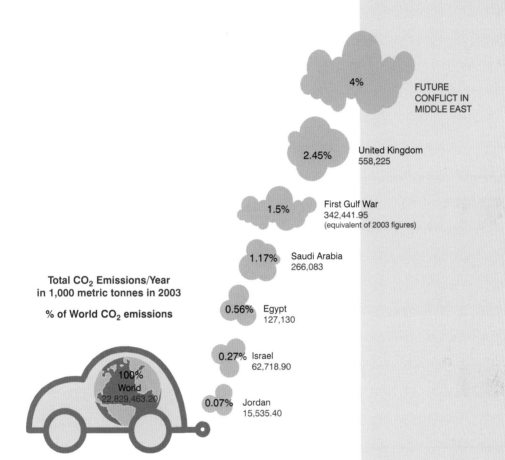

4%   FUTURE
      CONFLICT IN
      MIDDLE EAST

2.45%   United Kingdom
         558,225

1.5%   First Gulf War
        342,441.95
        (equivalent of 2003 figures)

1.17%   Saudi Arabia
         266,083

**Total CO_2 Emissions/Year
in 1,000 metric tonnes in 2003**

% of World CO_2 emissions

0.56%   Egypt
         127,130

0.27%   Israel
         62,718.90

100%
World
22,829,463.20

0.07%   Jordan
         15,535.40

The First Gulf war led to a 1.5% increase in world wide CO_2 emissions. In the case of a severe future conflict in the Middle East, CO_2 emissions could be double or triple, accounting for an increase of 3-5% of annual worldwide emissions. This would be more than the emissions of most of the Middle East in a normal year or more than the emissions of an industrialised country such as UK.

Cost of Conflict in the Middle East

7. LOSS OF BIO-DIVERSITY

The loss of marshlands in Iraq has had tremendous impact on biodiversity not only in the region but also beyond:

- Reduction of global biodiversity from Siberia to southern Africa
- Losses in fisheries in the northern Gulf, dependent on the marshlands for spawning grounds for the multi-million shrimp industry
- Extinction of mammals such as a sub-species of Otter and the Bandicoot Rat
- Threat to three unique endemic wetland bird species (Iraq Babbler, Basra Reed Warbler, Grey Hypocolius) and five endemic or near-endemic marshland sub-species (Little Grebe, African Darter, Black Francolin, White-eared Bulbul, Hooded Crow)
- Loss of agricultural land where rice and sugarcane were grown
- Increase in the salinity of the water and creation of crusts of salt on the ground
- Loss of the traditional homelands of the indigenous Ma'dan people.

This is merely an example of damage to biodiversity in one area in one period.

8. AGRICULTURE

Agricultural potential has suffered in all conflict zones in the region. The Palestinian Territories and Lebanon need to import food. The data on Iraq is not available.

Occupied Palestinian Territories

Commodities Imported

Wheat flour, sugar, oil, pulses, dairy products and meat/fish

Current problems, Future prospects

- Food insecurity is strongly correlated with the intensity of Israel's closure regime (severe restriction on freedom of movement).
- Palestinian controlled area is mainly urban with small area of agricultural use.
- Severe degradation of land due to ambiguity of land ownership, inaccessibility of land, lack of liquidity and cash, lack of economic motivations, limited education to farmers, lack of credit and marketing facilities.
- The declining quality of arable land and water.

Lebanon

Commodities Imported

Cereals, mainly wheat

Current problems, Future prospects

- The conflict in the summer of 2006 affected the agriculture sector directly, with crops, livestock and equipment damaged by the bombing.
- In Southern Lebanon, 25 per cent of agricultural fields and pastures have been rendered useless, until unexploded bombs can be removed.
- Approximately 3050 head of dairy cattle, 1250 bulls, 15000 goats and sheep, 18000 beehives and over 600000 broilers were lost as a direct consequence of the hostilities.
- Agricultural sector needs a huge infusion of investment to be able to capitalize on its potential. Due to continuing conflict and tensions, fiscal conditions make it difficult to raise significant amount of resources.

Cost of Conflict in the Middle East

The water stress in the Middle East is expected to be further exacerbated by climate change over the next decade. While climate change can not be directly ascribed to the atmosphere of conflict in the Middle East, it is likely to act as a threat multiplier – exacerbating water scarcity and tensions over water within and between nations. If there is no cooperation and collaboration between neighbouring countries that share water resources, the fight over natural resources could lead to a war.

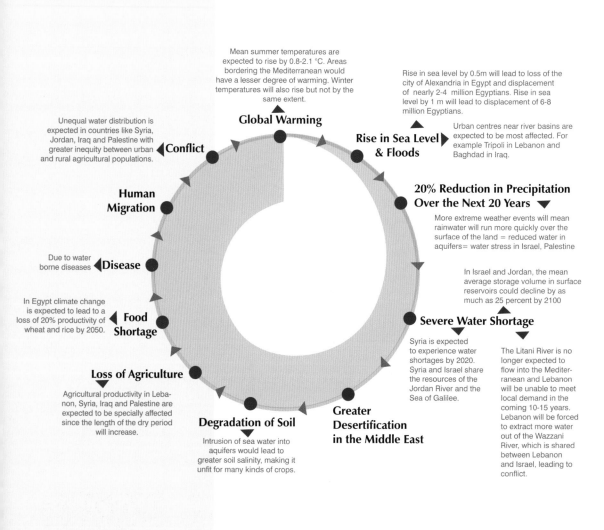

Mean summer temperatures are expected to rise by 0.8-2.1 °C. Areas bordering the Mediterranean would have a lesser degree of warming. Winter temperatures will also rise but not by the same extent.

Global Warming

Rise in sea level by 0.5m will lead to loss of the city of Alexandria in Egypt and displacement of nearly 2-4 million Egyptians. Rise in sea level by 1 m will lead to displacement of 6-8 million Egyptians.

Unequal water distribution is expected in countries like Syria, Jordan, Iraq and Palestine with greater inequity between urban and rural agricultural populations. **◀ Conflict**

Rise in Sea Level ▶ & Floods

Urban centres near river basins are expected to be most affected. For example Tripoli in Lebanon and Baghdad in Iraq.

Human Migration

20% Reduction in Precipitation Over the Next 20 Years ▼

More extreme weather events will mean rainwater will run more quickly over the surface of the land = reduced water in aquifers = water stress in Israel, Palestine

Due to water borne diseases **◀ Disease**

In Israel and Jordan, the mean average storage volume in surface reservoirs could decline by as much as 25 percent by 2100

In Egypt climate change is expected to lead to a loss of 20% productivity of wheat and rice by 2050. **◀ Food Shortage**

Severe Water Shortage ▼

Syria is expected to experience water shortages by 2020. Syria and Israel share the resources of the Jordan River and the Sea of Galilee.

The Litani River is no longer expected to flow into the Mediter-ranean and Lebanon will be unable to meet local demand in the coming 10-15 years. Lebanon will be forced to extract more water out of the Wazzani River, which is shared between Lebanon and Israel, leading to conflict.

Loss of Agriculture

Agricultural productivity in Leba-non, Syria, Iraq and Palestine are expected to be specially affected since the length of the dry period will increase.

Degradation of Soil ▼

Intrusion of sea water into aquifers would lead to greater soil salinity, making it unfit for many kinds of crops.

Greater Desertification in the Middle East

Chapter 4: Social & Political Costs

INTRODUCTION

The continuous persistence of conflicts in the Middle East and the presence of terrorist groups in the region have created the perception of it being a problem region. In reality, there are violent conflicts and terrorist groups in Latin America, Africa and Asia. The death toll caused by the Nepalese Maoists, Tamil Tigers, the FARC operatives in Colombia, Lord's Resistance Army in Uganda, and New People's Army in the Philippines in the last decade has been much more than that resulting from acts of violence and terror in the Middle East. Yet, the Middle East is associated with terror in the Western mind. Al Qaeda, which was clearly behind the 9/11 terrorist attacks and several attacks in Europe took birth in Afghanistan under the patronage of organs of the state in Pakistan. Yet the United States chooses to attack Iraq, threaten Iran, and effectively ignore the cause of the Palestinian people, while equipping the Pakistani army with F-16 aircrafts and more than a billion dollars of military aid. These discriminatory perspectives indicate the serious image problem the Arab societies have in the world.

The Gulf States have made impressive strides to develop the service sector and attract the best of human resources from around the world. Managers from multinational companies take postings there. Western universities have opened branches in Qatar and UAE. And yet, to an average American or European, Asia is hope and the Middle East is trouble. When the Western media talks about Asia, it recalls Bangalore and Shanghai and not Rangoon and Vientiane. On the other hand, the Middle East is symbolised by the strife in Basra and Beirut and not dynamism in Doha and Dubai.

Within the region, the context of conflict creates a sense of despair, promotes social orthodoxy, strengthens forces with absolutist vision and authoritarian tendencies, curbs innovation, and kills hope. Wars in the Middle East have destroyed children and intellectuals. There are no normal civil relations between common people in many countries. New fault-lines are emerging every few years. The fabric of human relations based on trust and decency has been weakened.

Cost of Conflict in the Middle East

Country by Governance : Peace & Violence   ■ Active Conflict

Presidential
   Egypt
   Syria

Parliamentary
   ■ Iraq
   ■ Israel
   ■ Lebanon
   ■ OPT

Theocracy
   ■ Iran

Monarchy
   Jordan
   Kuwait
   Qatar
   Saudi Arabia
   UAE

Religious Demography

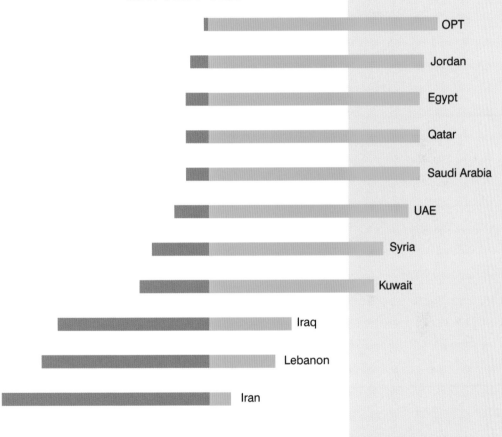

Shi'i / Others   Sunni

OPT

Jordan

Egypt

Qatar

Saudi Arabia

UAE

Syria

Kuwait

Iraq

Lebanon

Iran

Islamic   Jewish

Israel

Cost of Conflict in the Middle East

1. BREAKDOWN OF HUMAN INTERFACE

The Middle East was like a unified region for almost 400 years from 1517 to 1917. Despite wars between states, relations between families and communities flourished. Now the fabric of human relations has been torn apart.

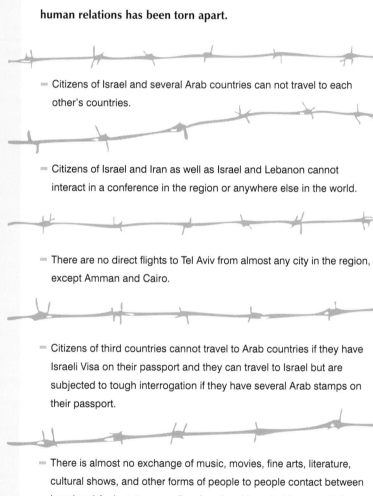

- Citizens of Israel and several Arab countries can not travel to each other's countries.

- Citizens of Israel and Iran as well as Israel and Lebanon cannot interact in a conference in the region or anywhere else in the world.

- There are no direct flights to Tel Aviv from almost any city in the region, except Amman and Cairo.

- Citizens of third countries cannot travel to Arab countries if they have Israeli Visa on their passport and they can travel to Israel but are subjected to tough interrogation if they have several Arab stamps on their passport.

- There is almost no exchange of music, movies, fine arts, literature, cultural shows, and other forms of people to people contact between Israel and Arab states as well as Israel and Iran. In this respect, the Middle East has particularly deprived itself of knowledge and happiness from interaction at the level of common citizens – the United States and the former Soviet Union during the Cold War, India and Pakistan, Japan and China, and other pairs of countries involved in hostile relations have not completely prevented their people from cultural exchanges.

2. RELIGION IN POLITICS

% of Seats in Parliament held by Religious Parties

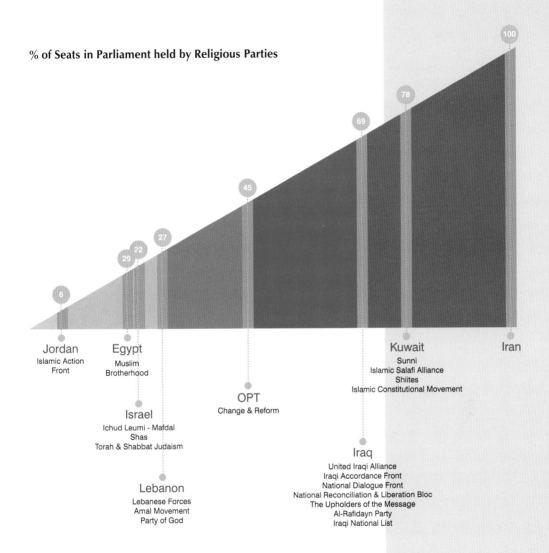

The conflict in the Middle East has made it easy for political groups and parties to mobilise people using religion. Iran remains fully theocratic 20 years after the revolution. Saudi Arabia's ruling structure is a partnership between the al-Saud family and the religious al-Shaikh family ever since the founding of the present state. In other countries, the number of legislators in Parliaments who are directly or indirectly associated with groups that advocate the role of religion has increased since 2003.

Cost of Conflict in the Middle East

3. FREEDOM OF PRESS

The Worldwide Press Freedom Index prepared by Reporters Without Borders ranks 169 states according to the degree of freedom of the press. The state with the highest degree of press freedom ranked 1 and the lowest ranked 169.

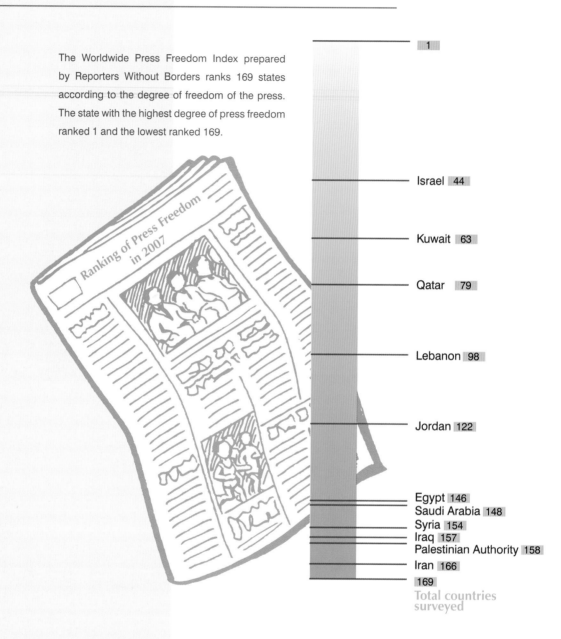

Ranking of Press Freedom in 2007

1	
Israel	44
Kuwait	63
Qatar	79
Lebanon	98
Jordan	122
Egypt	146
Saudi Arabia	148
Syria	154
Iraq	157
Palestinian Authority	158
Iran	166
169	

Total countries surveyed

Since the beginning of the decade the freedom of expression has been curbed in the Middle East - as reflected in the relative standing of countries in an index of press freedom. It is true that freedom of press is a function of authoritarian nature of governance. However, conflict provides justification for curbing the freedom of media. The United States asks its journalists covering Iraq to be 'embedded' with the military and imposes restrictions on what and how they can report. Thus, conflict may directly or indirectly impact press freedom.

4. CURBS ON CIVIL LIBERTIES

A protracted conflict breeds authoritarianism. It provides a good excuse to rulers to curb civil liberties and perpetuate their rule. Authoritarianism has its own life. It may find space due to historical, cultural, economic and social factors that may not be related to conflict. However, in the context of the Middle East, conflict has made it easy for regimes to introduce draconian laws and practices that restrict freedom.

EGYPT

- Remains subject to the Emergency Law since 1981.
- Law of Association
  - Prohibits the establishment of groups threatening the national unity
  - Restricts foreign funding of NGOs
  - Allows the Social Affairs Ministry to dissolve NGOs without a judicial order.
- The unified labour laws limit the unions' right to strike.
- Gender related laws discriminate against women in issuing passports and in inheritance laws.
- The government is involved in all academic and judicial appointments.
- The three leading daily newspapers are state controlled; editors are appointed by the President.
- Anti-Christian employment discrimination in the public sector, especially the security services and military.
- Members of the Baha'i faith are denied a range of civil documents, including identity cards, birth certificates and marriage licenses.
- Anti-Shiite sentiment on the rise.

IRAN

- Morality laws
  - Aimed at preventing 'social corruption'
  - Restrict the meeting of men and women in public
  - Enforce a strict Islamic dress code.
- The government controls all television and radio broadcasting; restricts any associations and publications that it deems harmful to the stability of the government.
- Conversion by Muslims to a non-Muslim religion is punishable by death.
- Minorities cannot hold senior or government positions, enjoy virtually no rights and are banned from practicing their faith.
- Several scholars have been beaten, detained and jailed for endangering national security and insulting Islam, which is a punishable under the law.

"laws discriminate against women"

"...state controlled newspapers"

"anti-Christian employment discrimination..."

"Muslims converting to a non-Muslim religion is punishable by death"

Cost of Conflict in the Middle East

- Independent labour unions are banned.
- Most number of juvenile executions.
- The penal code is based on Sharia and provides for flogging, stoning, amputation, and hanging for a range of social and political offences.
- Reports of torture in interrogations persist.
- Women face systematic discrimination in social and legal matters
  - Cannot obtain a passport without the permission of her husband or a male relative.
  - Do not enjoy equal rights under Sharia statutes governing divorce, inheritance, and child custody.
  - A woman's testimony in court is given only half the weight of a man's.

IRAQ

- Legislation passed in 2006 criminalized the ridicule of public officials; a number of Iraqi journalists have been charged with the offence.
- Broadcasters reporting on sectarian killings have been arrested for inciting violence.
- Freedom of Religion is guaranteed by the constitution. In reality, sectarian violence in Iraq targets nearly all religious communities and minority faiths.
- The lack of a legal framework and registration system for nongovernmental organizations hinders the NGOs' ability to function and attract donor funds.
- The Iraqi High Tribunal (IHT) statute does not explicitly require that guilt be proven beyond a reasonable doubt.
- The constitution promises women equal rights under the law. However, women who held jobs, attended university, or went out in public unveiled were frequently harassed, or even killed, by radical Islamist groups of both major sects.

ISRAEL

- Government authorities rely on Defence Regulations of 1945 to censor publications and mail, and restrict the movement of individuals.
- Arabs residing in East Jerusalem can be stripped of their Jerusalem residency if they remain outside the city for more than three months.
- More than half of the approximately 160,000 Negev Bedouins reside in unrecognized villages, which the state refuses to provide with a planning structure and place under municipal jurisdiction. They are under pressure to relocate to government-planned urban centres that completely disregard their traditional lifestyle.
- Journalists who travel to Arab countries such as Syria and Lebanon without government permission can and have been prosecuted.
- Increase in police brutality.

Margin notes:

"most number of juvenile executions"

"woman's testimony is given only half the weight of a man's"

"violence targets nearly all religious communities..."

"women... frequently harassed, or even killed..."

"journalists who travel ... without government permission can and have been prosecuted"

"increase in police brutality"

OCCUPIED PALESTINIAN TERRITORIES

- Palestinians under Israeli control in the West Bank and Gaza cannot vote in Israeli elections.
- Israel blocks journalists' access to active conflict zones, harasses Palestinian journalists.
- On several occasions during the latest Intifada, Israel prevented Muslim men under 45 from praying on the Temple Mount/Haram al-Sharif compound.
- Since 1967, over 10,000 houses have been demolished in OPT, including 2000 in East Jerusalem. Over 10,000 more houses are feared of being demolished in the future in East Jerusalem.
- There is enormous restriction on freedom of movement, as illustrated else where in this report.

JORDAN

- The king may dissolve the National Assembly and dismiss the cabinet at his discretion.
- Legislation criminalizes criticism of the royal family, slander of government officials, and speech that harms foreign relations, enflames religious sensitivities, or undermines the state's reputation.
- The parliament in 2006 approved a measure that allows only state-appointed councils to issue religious edicts, or fatwas, and makes it illegal to criticize these fatwas.
- Law on General Assemblies bans public demonstrations lacking written authorization from the regional governor.
- NGOs are prohibited from participating in political activity and workers must receive government permission to strike.
- Suspects may be detained for up to 48 hours without a warrant and up to 10 days without formal charges being filed; courts routinely grant prosecutors 15-day extensions of this deadline.
- Jordanians of Palestinian descent face discrimination in employment by the government and the military, and in admission to universities.

"Palestinians under Israeli control ... cannot vote"

"enormous restriction on freedom of movement"

"the King may dismiss the cabinet at his discretion"

"criminalizes criticism of the royal family"

"Palestinian descent face discrimination..."

Cost of Conflict in the Middle East

KUWAIT

"stateless residents... considered illegal residents, do not have full citizenship rights"

- The government imposes restrictions on freedom of assembly and association, although those rights are provided by law.
- The government restricts the registration and licensing of associations and nongovernmental organizations.
- Stateless residents, known as Bedouins (estimated 90,000 -130,000) are considered illegal residents, do not have full citizenship rights, live in wretched conditions.

LEBANON

"Palestinian refugees living in Lebanon are denied citizenship rights"

- A number of vaguely worded laws criminalize critical reporting on Syria, the military, the judiciary, and the presidency. General Security Directorate has the authority to censor all foreign media.
- Nearly 350,000 Palestinian refugees living in Lebanon are denied citizenship rights and face restrictions on working, building homes, and purchasing property.

SAUDI ARABIA

"religious freedom does not exist"

"academic freedom is restricted..."

"women are not treated as equal members of society"

- The royal family forbids the formation of political parties.
- The government tightly controls domestic media and dominates regional print and satellite television coverage.
- Religious freedom does not exist. Islam is the official religion. The government prohibits the public practice of any religions other than Islam and restricts the religious practices of both the Shiite and Sufi Muslim minority sects.
- Academic freedom is restricted; the teaching of Western philosophy and religions is banned.
- No freedom of association and assembly. Imprisonment and detainment of political activists who stage demonstrations or engage in other civic advocacy.
- Women are not treated as equal members of society. They are discriminated against with respect to travel, political representation, driving, and use of public spaces, education and crimes such as rape.

SYRIA

"freedom of expression is curtailed"

"public demonstrations are illegal without official permission"

- The only legal political party is the ruling Baath party and its several small coalition parties. A 2007 law restricts electoral transparency and monitoring.
- Freedom of expression is curtailed.
- The 2001 press law permits the authorities to deny or revoke publishing licenses and compels private print outlets to submit all material to government censors.
- Public demonstrations are illegal without official permission, usually granted only to pro-government groups.

- All non-worship meetings of religious groups require permits, and religious fund-raising is closely scrutinized.
- The government tightly monitors mosques and controls the appointment of Muslim clergy.
- All nongovernmental organizations require registration with the government; leaders of unlicensed human rights groups have frequently been jailed.
- Union activity is heavily controlled through the unified GFTU (General Federation of Trade Unions).
- Security agencies have unlimited authority to arrest suspects and hold them incommunicado for prolonged periods without charge. They extract confessions by torturing suspects and detaining their family members
- 200,000 Syrian Kurds are deprived of citizenship and unable to obtain passports, identity cards, or birth certificates, in turn preventing them from owning land, obtaining government employment, voting and travelling out of the country.
- Travel-ban on opposition figures, relatives of exiled dissidents, signers of the Beirut-Damascus Declaration, former Damascus Spring detainees, human rights lawyers, and their family members.
- Personal status law for Muslim women is governed by Sharia (Islamic law) and is discriminatory in marriage, divorce, and inheritance matters.

UAE

- All decisions about political leadership rest with the dynastic rulers of the seven emirates, who form the Federal Supreme Council, the highest executive and legislative body in the country.
- Restrictions on freedom of assembly and association. Small discussions on politics in private homes are tolerated, but there are limits on citizens' ability to organize broader gatherings.
- The new 2007 Labor Law does not give foreign workers the right to organize, bargain collectively, or strike.
- Although the constitution bans torture, Sharia courts sometimes impose flogging sentences for drug use, prostitution, and adultery.
- Discrimination against non-citizens occurs in many aspects of life, including employment, education, housing, and health care. Fewer than 20 percent of the country's residents are UAE citizens.
- Women's social, economic, and legal rights are not always protected because of incomplete implementation of the law and traditional biases against women.

"security agencies have unlimited authority to arrest suspects"

"200,000 Syrian Kurds are deprived of citizenship..."

"Personal status law for Muslim women... is discriminatory in marriage, divorce..."

"all decisions about political leadership rest with the dynastic rulers..."

"...fewer than 20 percent of the country's residents are UAE citizens"

Cost of Conflict in the Middle East

Iraq

1,350 + 800

children detained by military/police + multinational security forces

40%

internally displaced persons are children

30%

children are currently not attending school

40%

achieved a passing grade out of the 28% of the 17 year olds who gave the exams

760,000

children out of primary school

Large Number

deliberate targeting of educational establishments in 2007

Large Number

living outside Baghdad do not have access to water and sanitation

4%

under five do not survive

33%

of fatalities were children in July 2006 conflict

Lebanon

45%

displaced persons are children

20,000

children living in Nahar El Bared refugee camp

1,000,000

cluster bombs have exposed children to fatal risks

Large Number

of schools damaged in 2006

Palestine

1,000

children killed during 2000-2008

Many Incidents

of gun-firing in UNRWA schools by both IDF and Palestinian Groups

400

children under detention of Israeli authorities

Several

schools and hospitals burned and damaged every year

1,000s

of abductions of children by rival security forces

6. CONSCRIPTION

The Middle East is a region with the most widespread practice of compulsory conscription.

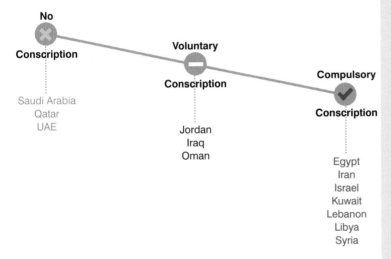

- Israel is a rare country to have compulsory conscription for women along with Cuba. Men are required to serve for 3 years and women for 2 years.

- In Israel, the right to conscientious objection is not legally recognized in the case of men. It is only partially recognized in the case of women under Article 39 of the National Defence Service Law.

- During the Iran-Iraq war (1980-1988) conscription took place at an unprecedented scale in both countries. In 1982 the armed forces consisted of 200,000 troops, but by 1988 one million men (about a quarter of Iraq's labour force) were under arms - the vast majority being conscripts. A further 700,000 civilians were recruited into temporary forces of the so-called Popular Army.

Cost of Conflict in the Middle East

7. SECTARIAN STRIFE

The conflict in the Middle East has deepened the sectarian divide. There were sectarian conflicts in Iraq prior to 2003. However, the war has prompted them to surface in an extremely violent way. Similarly, in Lebanon, Iran, Egypt and elsewhere in the region, sectarian differences have turned into violent clashes.

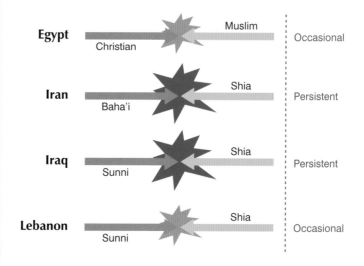

Multiple Fatality Bombings By Sectarian Groups in Iraq - 2007

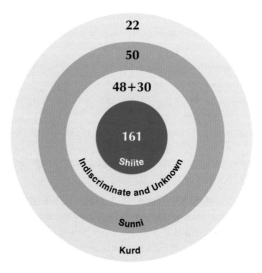

8. CRASH OF CIVILIZATION

Iraq is known as the cradle of Arabic civilization. It was attacked and destroyed twice – in 1257 by the Mongols and in 2003 by the Americans. The 2003 attack led to widespread looting which the new rulers of Baghdad could not control. Artefacts, books, manuscripts, and items of cultural importance have been stolen or damaged.

National Museum of Iraq, Baghdad

- The museum contains priceless relics from the Mesopotamian era, also known as the Cradle of Civilization, more than 5,000 years old.
- The museum remained closed from the First Gulf War I until 2000.
- Since April 2003 almost 15,000 items have been looted including coins, sculptures, ceramics, metalwork, architectural fragments, cuneiform tablets and most of the Museum's collection of valuable Sumerian cylindrical seals. Out of these about 5,000 items have been recovered, resulting in a net loss of 10,000 items.
- The stolen items include the famous alabaster "Warka Lady" dating from about 3100 BC; Bahrani's Sumerian statue, the gold-and-ivory carved plaque of a lioness attacking a Nubian, and the almost life-size head of the Goddess of Victory, from Hatra, made of copper.

Libraries and Archives

- National Library lost about half a million books.
- National Archives of Iraq lost documents from the Ottoman period.
- Al-Awqaf Library, part of the Ministry of Religious Affairs, lost over 5,000 Islamic manuscripts.
- The Central Library of the University of Baghdad lost about 600,000 printed books, serials and maps.
- Al-Mustansiriya University Library lost about 200,000 printed books.
- The library of Bayt al-Hikma was completely destroyed.

Destruction of ancient archaeological sites

- Satellite images show that archaeological sites equivalent in size to 3,000 football pitches have been dug up and plundered by looters.
- Entire cities such as the 5,000 year old city of Umma, cities of Bad-Tibra and Isin, have been pillaged and plundered.
- The American air base of Tallil outside Nasiriya in central Iraq is over the great Ziggurat of Ur, reputedly the earliest city on the earth. Ur is safe within the base compound. But its walls are pockmarked with wartime shrapnel and a blockhouse is being built over an adjacent archaeological site.
- Other reports indicate that the location of the great city of Babylon has been converted into a base for American troops, in the process of which a 2,500-year-old brick pavement to the Ishtar Gate was smashed by tanks and the gate itself damaged. Babylon is being rendered archaeologically barren.
- Outside the capital some 10,000 sites of incomparable importance to the history of civilization have been looted.

Cost of Conflict in the Middle East

The conflict in the Middle East has cost all countries in the region a serious dent in their global image.

In 2003, in a European Union poll, 59% of the Europeans cited Israel as the greatest threat to world security.

In 2007, in the Pew Global Attitudes Survey, Europeans expressed unfavourable opinion of Israel holding the Israelis responsible for the conflict with the Palestinians.

Opinion of People Polled on Israel-Palestine Conflict (in%)

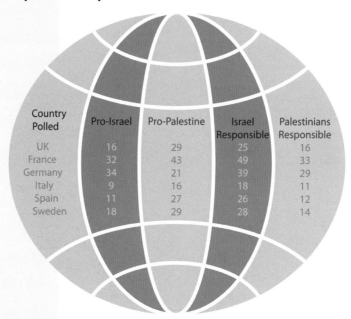

Country Polled	Pro-Israel	Pro-Palestine	Israel Responsible	Palestinians Responsible
UK	16	29	25	16
France	32	43	49	33
Germany	34	21	39	29
Italy	9	16	18	11
Spain	11	27	26	12
Sweden	18	29	28	14

It must be noted that the majority opinion the United States is favourable to Israel and holds the Palestinians responsible for conflict.

The opinion of Iran is negative across the board. In the 2007 Pew Global Attitudes Survey, the proportion of people who viewed Iran as somewhat unfavourable and very unfavourable was as follows.

France	84%
United States	71%
Canada	67%
Germany	85%

The conflict in the Middle East, 9/11 attacks, and the war in Iraq have weakened the fabric of trust between the Western and Islamic countries.

In 2007, the Pew Global Attitudes Survey included the most pro-West Arab countries and yet the divide was evident.

Pew Global Survey on Relations between the Muslim and Western Countries

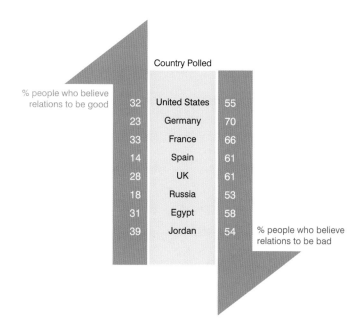

% people who believe relations to be good	Country Polled	% people who believe relations to be bad
32	United States	55
23	Germany	70
33	France	66
14	Spain	61
28	UK	61
18	Russia	53
31	Egypt	58
39	Jordan	54

Besides opinion polls, several other developments indicate the image of Arab nationals in the world. These include:

- Visa restrictions on Arab nationals
- Incidents like the Cartoon Crisis
- Resistance to strategic investments by Arab sources such as the Dubai Port
- Neglect of major Arab countries like Saudi Arabia in invitee list for G8 Outreach
- Negative depiction of Arab issues in the Western media
- Hate campaigns against Islamic countries in the Western universities.

Extraordinary attention

The Middle East has been the focus of extraordinary attention in international fora.

The Middle East (Palestine, Israel, Lebanon and Syria)

- represents 2 per cent of the 192 member states of the United Nations
- 0.5% of the world's population

In 2006, it was subject of

- 75.86 per cent of country specific General Assembly resolutions
- 100 per cent of resolutions from the Human Rights Council
- 13.5 per cent of Security Council resolutions.

Cost of Conflict in the Middle East

10. IRAQ'S CRISIS OF EDUCATION

Iraq has seen consistent decline in its education infrastructure since the 1970s. It is to some extent reflected in budgetary allocation for education.

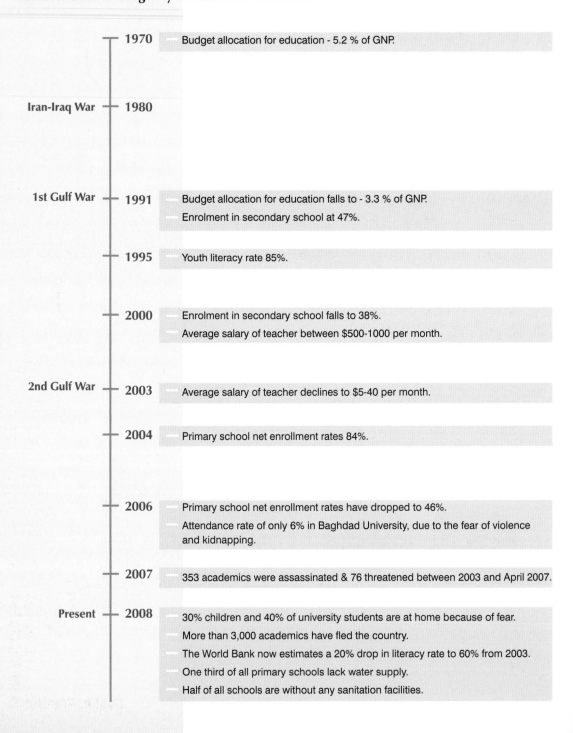

	1970	Budget allocation for education - 5.2 % of GNP.
Iran-Iraq War	1980	
1st Gulf War	1991	Budget allocation for education falls to - 3.3 % of GNP.
		Enrolment in secondary school at 47%.
	1995	Youth literacy rate 85%.
	2000	Enrolment in secondary school falls to 38%.
		Average salary of teacher between $500-1000 per month.
2nd Gulf War	2003	Average salary of teacher declines to $5-40 per month.
	2004	Primary school net enrollment rates 84%.
	2006	Primary school net enrollment rates have dropped to 46%.
		Attendance rate of only 6% in Baghdad University, due to the fear of violence and kidnapping.
	2007	353 academics were assassinated & 76 threatened between 2003 and April 2007.
Present	2008	30% children and 40% of university students are at home because of fear.
		More than 3,000 academics have fled the country.
		The World Bank now estimates a 20% drop in literacy rate to 60% from 2003.
		One third of all primary schools lack water supply.
		Half of all schools are without any sanitation facilities.

11. EDUCATION COSTS OF LEBANON'S 2006 WAR

Lebanon - July 2006 War

300
schools partially damaged

50
schools destroyed

40,000
education disrupted

Furthermore:

- A large number of children had to travel longer distances to go to school because their schools were destroyed or damaged.
- Teachers reported that many children were psychologically scarred by the turmoil of war.
- Several families were displaced from their homes thus making it even harder to continue with the day to day realities of school and academics.
- An assessment of 45 schools in 4 rural districts in Lebanon revealed that there was a high rate of aggression and attention problems amongst students between November 2006 and March 2007. It also revealed a significant drop in grades in the summer following the July 2006 war.

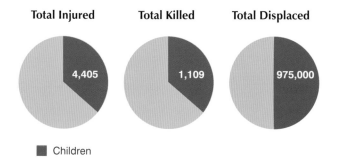

Total Injured	Total Killed	Total Displaced
4,405	1,109	975,000

■ Children

Cost of Conflict in the Middle East

12. CULTURE OF VIOLENCE

In a normal human society, people seek peace, friendship and trust in enlightened self interest. In a society ravaged by the culture of violence, there are primary indicators of debasement of human life. There are also secondary indicators which may not be directly linked to conflict but which easily surface because of the context of violence and despair. The indicators identified here are illustrative and not exhaustive.

Substance abuse and addiction   Psychological trauma   Fear driven by rumours

Feeling of vulnerability and uncertainty   Trafficking of women   Rape

Revenge mentality   Segregation of communities   Honour killings

Missing persons   Hardening of positions   Erosion of institutions

Miscarriage of justice   Torture   Domestic violence

Eulogising of death by violence   Demonising the "other"

Rise of militias   Growth of extremist groups and cults

Suicide bombings   Daily killings of civilians

Gun culture   Abductions   Curbs on freedom

Use of violence to settle personal scores

Indoctrination of children for conscription and martyrdom

Radicalisation of society

Polarisation of the media

Skewed textbooks

Intolerance

Chapter 5 : Costs for the Palestinian People

INTRODUCTION

Ever since the birth of Israel, the conflict over a homeland for the Palestinian people has dominated the politics of the Middle East. The Oslo Accords provided hope for constructing a two-state solution in the early 1990s. However, the failure of the Camp David Summit in 2002 has given rise to the Second Intifada. Since September 29, 2000, Israel and the Palestinian groups have been engaged in an ongoing violent confrontation, a sequel to the first Intifada that had lasted from approximately 1988 to 1992.

Israel and the Arab states have proposed counter-initiatives for resolving the Palestinian conflict – i.e. the Israeli Disengagement Plan and the Arab League Peace Plan. Neither finds favour with the other side. The international community in the form of the United Nations and the Quartet have also failed to find a solution, which can be acceptable to the two sides.

For the first five decades, from 1948 to 1998, the Palestinians were primarily represented by the Palestine Liberation Organisation (PLO). In the last ten years, in addition to the Fatah, the main constituent of the PLO, Hamas has emerged as a representative organisation of the Palestinian people. It has won elections for the Palestinian Authority. However, Israel describes it as a terrorist organisation and therefore refuses to negotiate with it since the Hamas Covenant of 1998 vows to eliminate the state of Israel. The Arab societies consider Hamas a legitimate representative organisation and negotiating agent of the Palestinian people. As a result, there is a deadlock.

In terms of the number of deaths and economic indicators, the Palestinian conflict is much smaller than some of the other conflicts in the Middle East. In terms of emotional value, it is at the core of the politics and conflict in the region. The resolution of the Palestinian conflict can pave way for comprehensive and sustainable peace in the region.

Cost of Conflict in the Middle East

This map represents the Palestinian version and includes East Jerusalem – Israel may disagree with it since it does not consider East Jerusalem as an occupied territory.

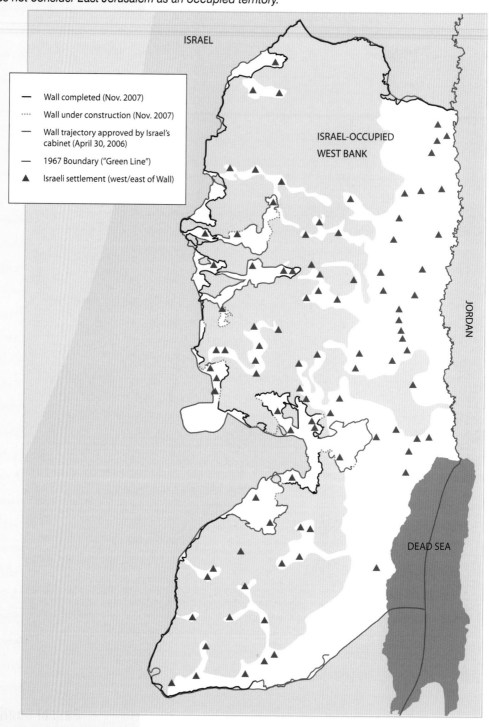

1. HUMAN COSTS

Palestinian fatalities since the beginning of the Intifada (2000)

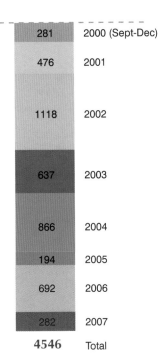

281	2000 (Sept-Dec)
476	2001
1118	2002
637	2003
866	2004
194	2005
692	2006
282	2007
4546	Total

Deaths due to Hamas-Fatah fighting

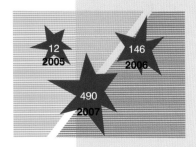

12 2005

146 2006

490 2007

Number of Palestinians in Israeli Detention Centres – April 2007

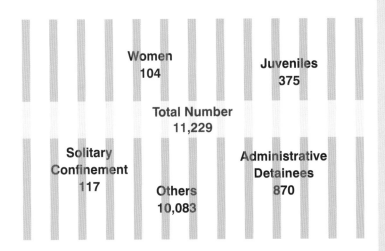

Women
104

Juveniles
375

Total Number
11,229

Solitary
Confinement
117

Others
10,083

Administrative
Detainees
870

Cost of Conflict in the Middle East

Official and deep poverty among individuals and households in Palestine

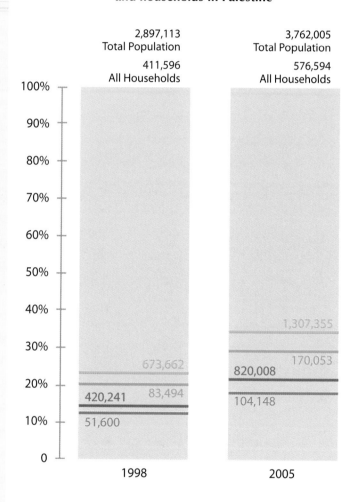

Official Poor Persons
Official Poor Households
Deep Poor Persons
Deep Poor Households

In 1998, the Palestinian National Commission for Poverty Alleviation defined two poverty lines—official poverty and deep poverty—on the basis of actual average consumption expenditures of Palestinian households.

Official poverty line = per day per capita $2.4
Deep poverty line = per day per capita $2.0
(based on exchange rates in 2004)

The number of people in deep poverty in 2006 increased to more than 1 million.

3. ISRAELI SETTLEMENTS

Growth of Settler Population 1991-2007

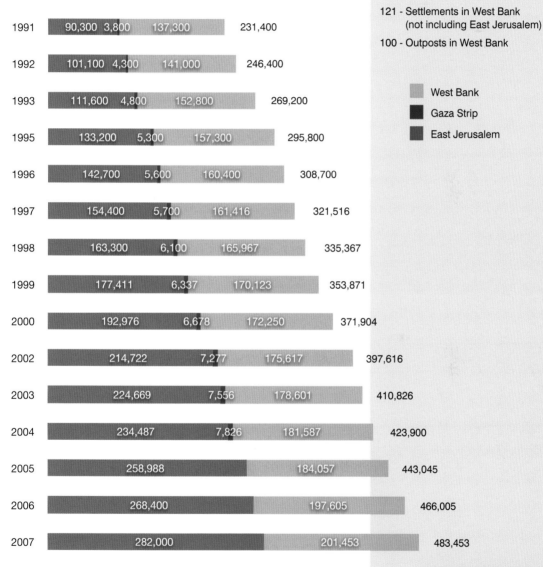

Year				Total
1991	90,300	3,800	137,300	231,400
1992	101,100	4,300	141,000	246,400
1993	111,600	4,800	152,800	269,200
1995	133,200	5,300	157,300	295,800
1996	142,700	5,600	160,400	308,700
1997	154,400	5,700	161,416	321,516
1998	163,300	6,100	165,967	335,367
1999	177,411	6,337	170,123	353,871
2000	192,976	6,678	172,250	371,904
2002	214,722	7,277	175,617	397,616
2003	224,669	7,556	178,601	410,826
2004	234,487	7,826	181,587	423,900
2005	258,988		184,057	443,045
2006	268,400		197,605	466,005
2007	282,000		201,453	483,453

121 - Settlements in West Bank
(not including East Jerusalem)

100 - Outposts in West Bank

- West Bank
- Gaza Strip
- East Jerusalem

Cost of Conflict in the Middle East

Number of hospitals, beds and beds per 1,000 population in the Palestinian Territory in mid year by region 1996-2005:

West Bank

	1996	2000	2005
No. of Hospitals	31	48	54
Beds per 1000 population	1.2	1.2	1.3

Gaza Strip

	1996	2000	2005
No. of Hospitals	6	17	22
Beds per 1000 population	0.92	1.6	1.4

Palestinian Territories

	1996	2000	2005
No. of Hospitals	37	65	76
Beds per 1000 population	1.1	1.4	1.3

- Some 42.1% of the Palestinian households in localities affected by the separation wall have problems of access to health services.

- Of some 4,074 patients in Gaza who applied for travel permits on medical grounds between June-Nov. 2007, 713 have had their applications denied.

- As of May 2007, the level of anaemia among children 0-9 months old stood at 72.2% in Gaza and 45% in the West Bank.

- As a result of fuel and electricity restrictions imposed in 2007, Gaza hospitals experienced power cuts for 8-12 hours a day. In 2008, there was a 60-70% shortage reported in the diesel required for hospital power generators.

5. A SPLIT WIDE OPEN

The most devastating impact of conflict has been the breakdown of the Palestinian institutions.

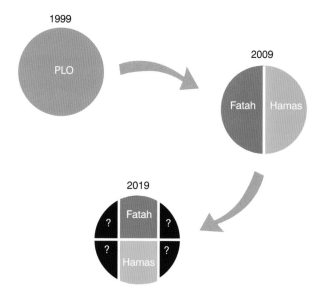

The ideological split has led to territorial division of spheres of influence, dissolution of an elected government, difficulties in the electoral process and lack of effective political authority.

Child fatalities by circumstances since the beginning of the Intifada
(Sept 2000 - June 2007)

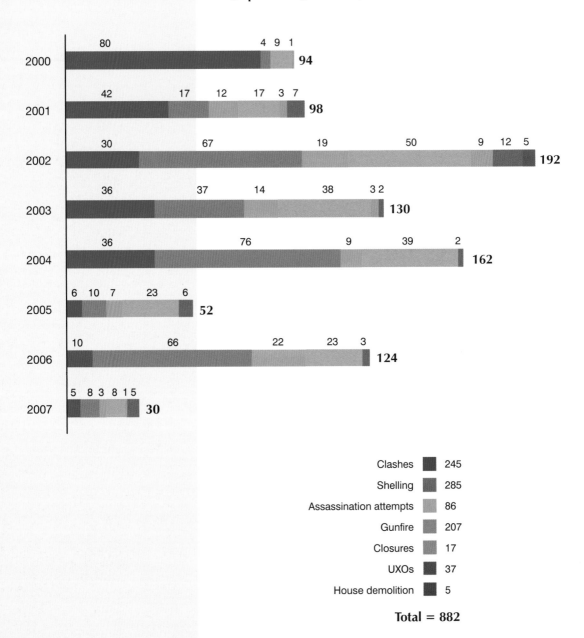

Clashes	245
Shelling	285
Assassination attempts	86
Gunfire	207
Closures	17
UXOs	37
House demolition	5

Total = 882

7. EDUCATION LOST

More than 40
Palestinian schools occupied by the Israeli Defence Forces, since 2000

More than 2,000
School drop-outs in Gaza in the second half of 2007

More than 3,000
School children detained by Israeli Defence forces since 2000

Innumerable
School children turned back from check-points since 2000

Cancellation of
IT, Science Labs, Extra-curricular Activities due to high energy consumption

Rapid decrease
Net enrollment ratio for primary schooling

More than 1,300
Schools disrupted by curfews, sieges, closures

More than 10%
of children in Gaza have witnessed the killing of a teacher in school

Half of the students
have seen their school besieged by troops

One third
of families experience anxiety, phobias or depression

Cost of Conflict in the Middle East

Damage Caused to Gaza Farmers Due to Israeli Practices
(Sep. 28th, 2000 through Dec. 31st, 2006)

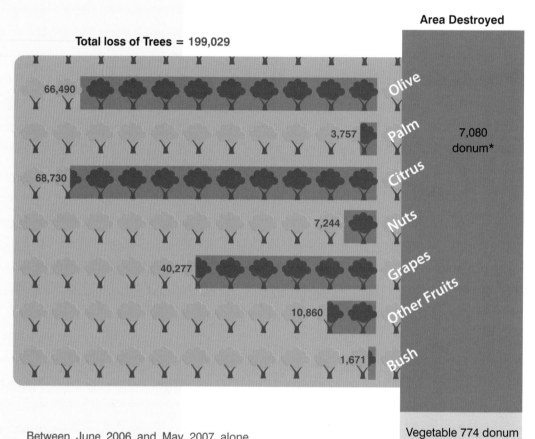

Area Destroyed

Total loss of Trees = 199,029

66,490 — Olive

3,757 — Palm

68,730 — Citrus

7,244 — Nuts

40,277 — Grapes

10,860 — Other Fruits

1,671 — Bush

7,080 donum*

Vegetable 774 donum

Greenhouses 49 donum — Field Crops 182 donum

Total Area = 8,085 donum

Between June 2006 and May 2007 alone, Israeli forces destroyed some 12,900 donums of agricultural land (WB:6,700; GS:6,200) and 322 greenhouses (WB: 155; GS:167), and uprooted 2,775 trees in the West Bank.

* A Donum is a unit of area used in many countries formerly part of the Ottoman Empire, equivalent to 1,000 square meters

Estimated Direct Loss Incurred by Farmers
(Sep 28th, 2000 through Dec 31st, 2006)

Governorate : Gaza (loss in $)

Bulldozing lands, trees, vegetables, and greenhouses	42,846,895
Bulldozing assets and wells and killing of animals and birds	7,070,178
Other damage including fishermen tools	374,836
Total Loss	50,291,909

The indirect loss in the Gaza Strip and the West Bank reached $828,926,225. These were mainly incurred due to the following:

- Loss in the olive sector and stealing of agricultural crops
- Low processing of agricultural products (animals and plants)
- Loss in the animal sector
- Loss in the fishery sector
- High prices of fodder
- Loss in export to Israel and abroad
- Prevention of agricultural movement
- Loss due to reduction of agricultural workers
- Loss due to bulldozing the land

Affected population: There are no clear statistics reporting number of affected households and farmers. However, the agricultural sector in the Gaza strip employs some 40,000 workers and supports 25% of the Gaza Strip households.

Cost of Conflict in the Middle East

Number of Palestinians Employed 2005 : 633,000

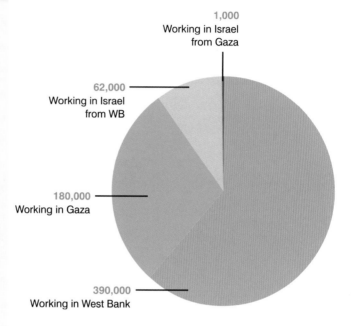

1,000
Working in Israel
from Gaza

62,000
Working in Israel
from WB

180,000
Working in Gaza

390,000
Working in West Bank

Dependency Ratio

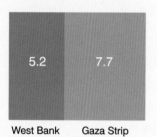

5.2	7.7
West Bank	Gaza Strip

Palestinian workers in Israeli Settlements

(% of total Palestinian workers)

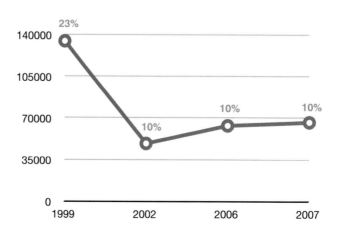

23%
140000

105000

10%

70000
10%

10%

35000

0

1999   2002   2006   2007

10. JOBLESS IN GAZA

Employment

37.6%
unemployment in 2007, set to rise to 50%

53%
total employment in private sector

75,000
lost jobs out of a total labour force of 110,000 due to bankruptcies

95%
Gaza's industrial operations are suspended due to import-export ban

Industry

 Raw materials, non-humanitarian commercial goods, and essential equipment for sewage system and water network repairs not allowed to enter Gaza since June 12, 2007

1,750
people employed by 195 factories in June 2007. A drop from 35,000 people employed by 3,900 factories in June 2005

3,500
jobs lost due to shut down of all 438 construction factories in Gaza (Nov 2007)

Agriculture

40,000
workers who depended on cash crops now have no income

 Farmers cannot export their crops

Cost of Conflict in the Middle East

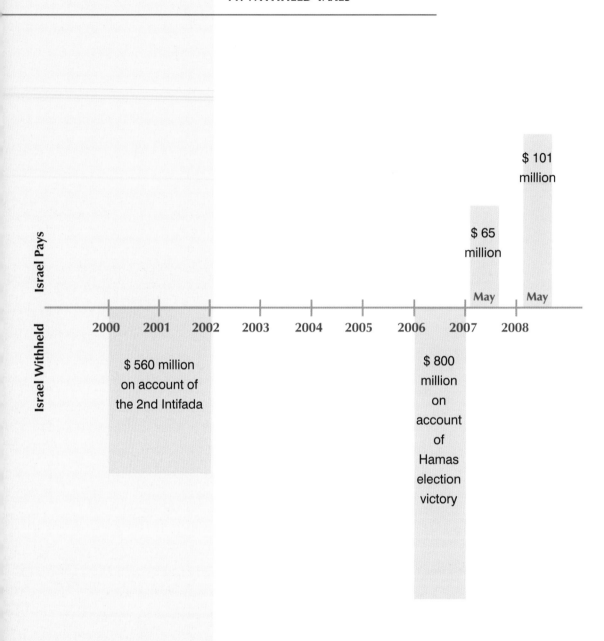

Israel Pays

Israel Withheld

$ 101 million

$ 65 million

May   May

2000   2001   2002   2003   2004   2005   2006   2007   2008

$ 560 million on account of the 2nd Intifada

$ 800 million on account of Hamas election victory

12. BARRIERS AND CLOSURES

Number of Closures : (days per year)

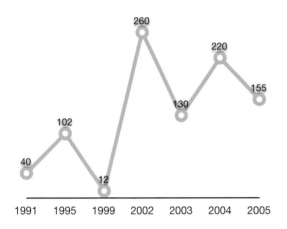

During closure days, no Palestinians are allowed to travel to Israel, as these days render their work, trade, travel permits invalid. Even though reliable data for 2006-2008 was not available, scattered news reports indicated the same trends as the previous three years, (2003-2005).

Checkpoints

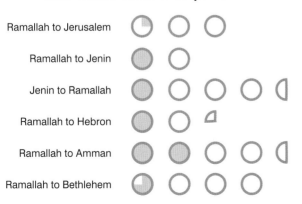

○ Check-points
○ Flying check-points

Time Wasted due to Checkpoints

Ramallah to Jerusalem
Ramallah to Jenin
Jenin to Ramallah
Ramallah to Hebron
Ramallah to Amman
Ramallah to Bethlehem

— Time with Check-points
— Time without Check-points
○ = 1 hour

Cost of Conflict in the Middle East

- Palestinians who own land or property in the Jordan Valley but live in the West Bank can no longer access the area without a special permit. Permits do not allow overnight stay. Waiting times at Jordan Valley checkpoints range between 30 and 90 minutes.

- In Nablus governorate, villagers from 'Asira ash Shamaliya have had to use the more circuitous Al Badhan road to access Nablus (a 30-minute journey) because of the closure of the traditional route (a 10-minute journey). The almost continual presence of a flying checkpoint on the Al Badhan Road, involving delays of an hour or more, triples the time taken to reach the city.

- It is estimated that 50% of the total West Bank is currently restricted area and Palestinians are restricted from 41 sections of roads in WB. Vehicles bearing Palestinian license plates are forbidden or restricted on 312km of main roads in the WB as compared with some 1,661km of roads in the WB that are primarily for Israeli use.

Man-hours Wasted due to Checkpoints

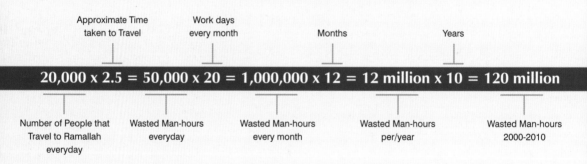

Palestinian Deaths Due to Delay in Medical Treatment

- 51 Palestinians died between 2000-2007.

- According to WHO, the proportion of patients given permits to exit Gaza for medical care decreased from 89.3% in January 2007 to 64.3% in December 2007.

- During the period October to December 2007, WHO has confirmed the deaths of 20 patients, including 5 children. Between 2007-2008, 120 people in Gaza died because they were not allowed to access medical treatment in Egypt.

13. WEST BANK WALL

The West Bank Barrier (Wall) at a glance
(As of April 2008)

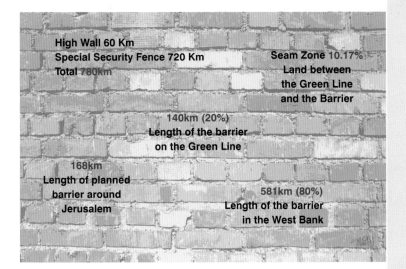

High Wall 60 Km
Special Security Fence 720 Km
Total 780km

Seam Zone 10.17%
Land between
the Green Line
and the Barrier

140km (20%)
Length of the barrier
on the Green Line

168km
Length of planned
barrier around
Jerusalem

581km (80%)
Length of the barrier
in the West Bank

Israel has declared land that falls in between the route of the barrier and the greenline as the 'seam zone'. Palestinians who fall within this zone are required to seek permission from Civil Administration to remain in their homes and have access to their own property. About 50,000 Palestinians live in the seam zone. In addition there is a 'buffer zone' of 150-200m adjacent to the wall on the east side where Palestinian construction is not allowed.

Cost of Conflict in the Middle East

14. DEMOLITION OF HOUSES

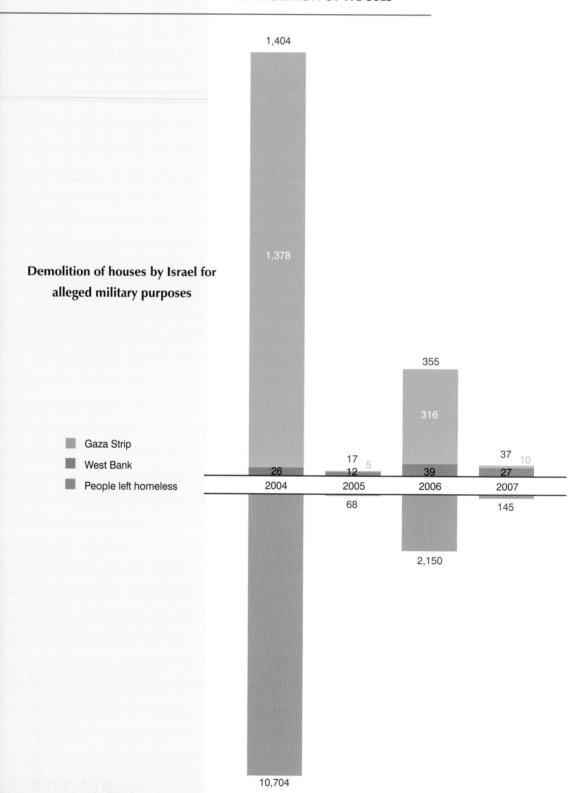

Demolition of houses by Israel for alleged military purposes

Gaza Strip
West Bank
People left homeless

1,404

1,378

355

316

17
12   5

37   10

26

39

27

2004   2005   2006   2007

68

145

2,150

10,704

15. IDENTITY CARDS

Number of Identity Cards Revoked

Year	Cards Revoked
2000	207
2003	272
2004	16
2005	222
2006	1,363

Cards Revoked
8,269
Since 1967

Cost of Conflict in the Middle East

UNRWA Registered Refugees – (RRs) (June 2007)

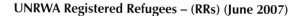

■ West Bank ■ Gaza Strip ■ Jordan ■ Syria ■ Lebanon

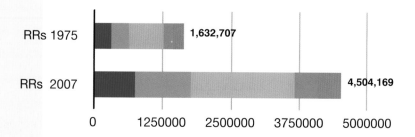

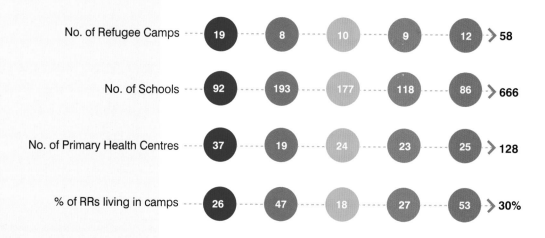

The total 1948 refugee population was estimated at approximately 6 million in 2007, including 4.5 million registered with UNRWA and 1.5 million not registered.

Around half of the Palestinians in the Occupied Territories, including most of the people in Gaza, are refugees.

17. BLACK-OUT IN GAZA

Gaza Power Plant Power Generating Capacity in MW

140 - Original capacity

80 - Post June 2006 bombing

65 - Post Israeli restriction on fuel supplies
imposed in September 2007

Palestinian Dependence on Israel for Electricity : November 2007

	Mega Watts	Controlled by	
West Bank			
Maximum Limit: 550MW			
Supplied Directly by IEC (Israeli Electrical Co.)	165MW	Israel	30%
Supplied Indirectly by IEC through JEDCO	385MW	Israel	70%
Gaza Strip			
Maximum Limit: 202 MW			
Supplied by Gaza Power Generating Company (GPGC)	65MW	Israel	91%
Supplied by IEC	120MW	Israel	
Supplied by Egyptian Electrical Company	17MW	Egypt	9%

The WB depends almost entirely on the Israeli Electricity Co. (IEC) for electricity supply. It has no generation capacity or transmission network.

Cost of Conflict in the Middle East

Water for Agriculture in Israel and Palestine

Israel
Palestine

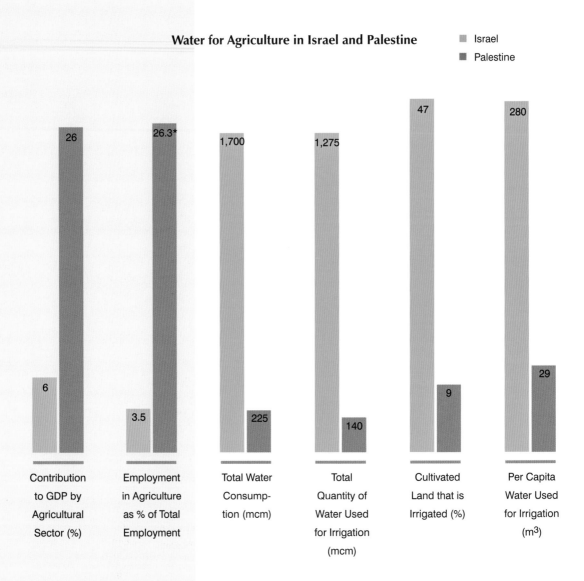

* Excludes Palestinians working in Israel

Chapter 6 : Costs to Israel

INTRODUCTION

Israel has a superior military might and a strong support of the world's leading power, the United States. Nevertheless, it is also vulnerable. It failed to achieve its objective of defeating Hezbollah in the summer of 2006. On the other hand, it suffered severe human and economic damage in the conflict.

In addition, Israel is subjected to regular attacks from the Palestinian groups. The withdrawal from Gaza has made no difference. These include missile attacks, suicide bombing and other forms of bombings. Israeli adults, youth and children and have been killed in these attacks.

Israel also pays a huge cost in the form of economic opportunity as a result of its hostility with the Arab states. It has to look for distant sources for its energy needs, when Gaza has significant natural gas reserves and Gulf States are the main suppliers of oil to the world. Its scope for tourism, trade and investments in the region has narrowed.

Moreover, the present President of Iran threatens to wipe Israel out evoking emotions of extremist elements in the region.

Finally, the conflict has created a context of insecurity, mistrust and fear for the people of Israel. It is a context in which normal human relationships are rendered difficult and human values are undermined.

Cost of Conflict in the Middle East

Israel's Key Strategic Concerns in 2009

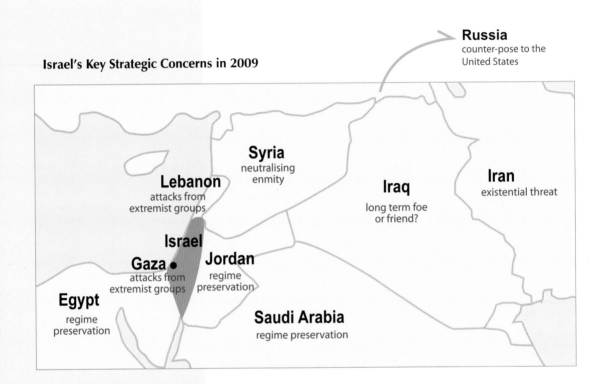

1. HUMAN COSTS

Israeli casualties in battle since 1948 : 22396 Total

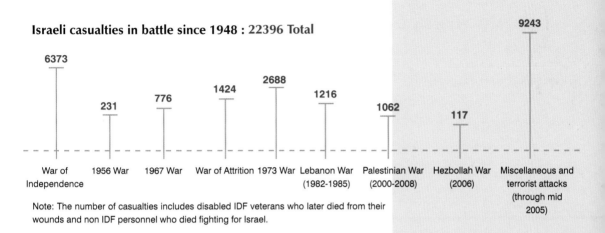

6373		
	9243	

War of Independence — 6373
1956 War — 231
1967 War — 776
War of Attrition — 1424
1973 War — 2688
Lebanon War (1982-1985) — 1216
Palestinian War (2000-2008) — 1062
Hezbollah War (2006) — 117
Miscellaneous and terrorist attacks (through mid 2005) — 9243

Note: The number of casualties includes disabled IDF veterans who later died from their wounds and non IDF personnel who died fighting for Israel.

Statistical overview of members of bereaved families

Widows	Bereaved Parents (couples)	Single Bereaved Parents	Orphans	Disabled Veterans
3285	4029	4457	2167	79239

Note: These figures represent 'destroyed families' – those that have lost fathers, mothers, brothers, sisters and children.

Number of Israeli civilians and Security Force Personnel killed since al-Aqsa Intifada (29 September 2000 – 31 March 2008)

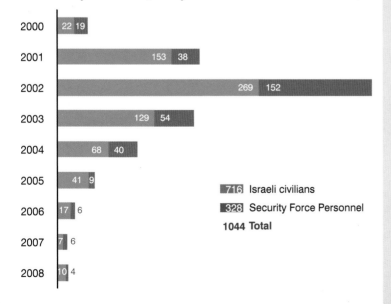

Year	Israeli civilians	Security Force Personnel
2000	22	19
2001	153	38
2002	269	152
2003	129	54
2004	68	40
2005	41	9
2006	17	6
2007	7	6
2008	10	4

716 Israeli civilians
328 Security Force Personnel
1044 Total

Cost of Conflict in the Middle East

2. CAFES, SCHOOLS AND BOMBS

Young Israelis, especially students have been targeted by bombers. Cafes, discos, pubs and malls, areas where young people hang out have proved to be popular targets of terrorists and suicide bombers. This has created an atmosphere of fear and insecurity which has limited children's ability to move about, to attend school and to participate in social, cultural, religious and other events.

Israeli minors* killed since the al-Aqsa Intifada:
29 September 2000 to 31 March 2008

Year	Occupied Territories	Israel
2000	0	0
2001	10	26
2002	20	27
2003	1	20
2004	4	4
2005	3	3
2006	1	0
2007	0	0
2008	0	4
Total	39	84

*upto the age of 18

Illustrations of attacks on children and youth

Mercaz Harav Yeshiva (school), Jerusalem
2008

School Bus, Jerusalem
2004

"Mike's Place" (Pub), Tel Aviv
2003

London Cafe, Netanya
2003

Cafe Hillel, Emek Refaim St.
2003

Maxim (restaurant), Haifa
2003

School Bus, Jerusalem
2002

Shopping mall, Kfar Sava
2002

School Bus, Jerusalem
2002

Student cafeteria, Hebrew University
2002

School, Netanya
2001

Disco, Tel Aviv
2001

School Bus Kfar Darom
2000

School Bus Gush Katif
1998

The school system is not managing to 'hold onto' its pupils, and loses more than 20,000 dropouts from each graduating class.

The dropout rate from 8th to 10th Grade is 8.5 percent among the Jews and 11.2 percent among the Arabs.

Immediately after the war with Lebanon, 55,000 children were diagnosed with different levels of anxiety syndromes.

3. MISSILE ATTACKS

Israel is vulnerable to missile attacks – particularly Qassam rockets and mortars.
If the attacks continue at the same rate as in the first seven years of this decade,
Israel could possibly face almost 47,000 missile attacks during 2000-2010.

Year	Total Missile Attacks	Qassam Missile Attacks
2000	2783	-
2001	7634	4
2002	5371	35
2003	4439	155
2004	4849	231
2005	3073	179
2006	2955	946
2007	2946	783
Total 2000-2007	34050	2333

Cost of Conflict in the Middle East

4. FEAR PSYCHOSIS

The National Resilience Project of the University of Haifa (2004) shows that Israeli citizens of all types are fearful of terror attacks. In a survey conducted by the project, the investigators found out that more than 90% respondents in all categories were worried about terrorist attacks.

Israelis Fearful of Terrorist Attacks

1. Marital Status

Single 91.85%   Married 91.55%

2. Gender

Male 87.30%   Female 95.72%

3. Couples

With Children 91.86%   Without Children 91.97%

4. Level of Education

With Elementary Education 87.61%
With High School   91.84%
With post High School (non-academic)   93.96%
With post High School (academic)   91.42%

5. Religiosity

Secular   92.57%   Traditional   91.61%
Religious   89.44%   Orthodox   93.27%

6. Income

With much > Average Income   88.67%
With > Average Income   92.01%
With Average Income   92.96%
With < Average Income   91.75%
With much < Average Income   92.02%

7. Residence in West Bank

Living in West Bank   94%
Not living in West Bank   93.31%

8. Immigrant Status

New Immigrants from former Soviet Union   96.06%
Veteran Immigrants from former Soviet Union   93.77%

9. Jews or Arab Residents

Jews   94.03%

Arabs 80.70%

Moreover, according to an opinion poll, 37% of Israeli youth fear another Holocaust.

5. ECONOMIC DAMAGE

The impact of the al-Aqsa Intifada on Israel's Economic indicators

○ Unemployment rate %

◎ GDP annual % change

◌ Inflation, average consumer prices (annual % change)

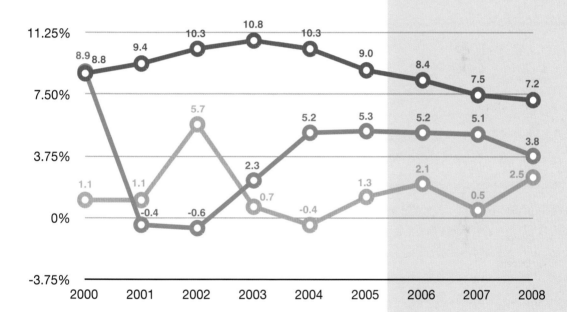

Israel's engagement in conflict has a direct impact on the country's economic growth. Following the start of the al-Aqsa Intifada in September 2000, unemployment levels increased in 2001 and continued to rise till 2003. Although there was a downward trend from 2004, levels continued to remain above the 2000 rates until 2006. Furthermore, Israel experienced a reduction in GDP levels in the years following the start of the second Intifada. In conjunction, 2002 saw the lowest GDP levels in recent times, coupled with the highest rate of inflation, both of which coincided with a spate of suicide bombings.

Cost of Conflict in the Middle East

6. BATTLEGROUND EXPERIENCE FOR THE BIG BOSS

It is almost compulsory for every Israeli Prime Minister to have military background. Every head of the Israeli government has had military or intelligence experience. With the exception of Prime Minister Ehud Olmert, all Israeli Prime Ministers since Yitzhak Rabin have held the post of Minister of Defence and/or Minister of Foreign Affairs. It appears impossible for a civilian politician to reach the top slot in a representative democracy.

Military backgrounds of Israeli Prime Ministers: 1970s to Present

Prime Minister	Tenure	Party	Military Career	
			Enlisted	Service Years & Rank
Yitzhak Rabin	1974 - 1977 & 1992 - 1995	Labour	√	27yrs Chief of Staff
Menachem Begin	1977 - 1983	Likud	√	Commander of IZL*
Yitzhak Shamir	1983 - 1984 & 1986 - 1992	Likud	√	10yrs Mossad
Shimon Peres	1984 - 1986	Kadima	√	6yrs DG MOD & Haganah**
Benjamin Netanyahu	1996 - 1999	Likud	√	5yrs Special Forces
Ehud Barak	1999 - 2001	Labour	√	36yrs Lt.General
Airel Sharon	2001 - 2006	Likud/Kadima	√	26yrs Major General
Ehud Olmert	2006 - 2008	Kadima	√	Infantry Officer

Note : * Irgun Zeva'l Le'umi - National Military Organisation
** Haganah - Jewish paramilitary, which evolved into Israel Defence Force

7. IMAGE LOSS

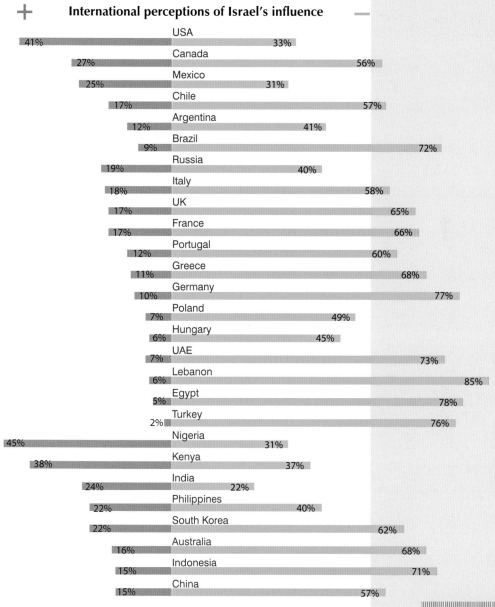

International perceptions of Israel's influence + —

Country	+	—
USA	41%	33%
Canada	27%	56%
Mexico	25%	31%
Chile	17%	57%
Argentina	12%	41%
Brazil	9%	72%
Russia	19%	40%
Italy	18%	58%
UK	17%	65%
France	17%	66%
Portugal	12%	60%
Greece	11%	68%
Germany	10%	77%
Poland	7%	49%
Hungary	6%	45%
UAE	7%	73%
Lebanon	6%	85%
Egypt	5%	78%
Turkey	2%	76%
Nigeria	45%	31%
Kenya	38%	37%
India	24%	22%
Philippines	22%	40%
South Korea	22%	62%
Australia	16%	68%
Indonesia	15%	71%
China	15%	57%

Note : The results were obtained by a poll conducted on 28,000 people across 27 countries by the Program on International Policy Attitudes (PIPA) for the BBC Word Service.

Cost of Conflict in the Middle East

- The Director of PIPA, Steven Kull, stated that it appeared "...that people around the world tend to look negatively on countries whose profile is marked by the use or pursuit of military power. This includes Israel..."
- 23 of the 27 surveyed countries viewed Israel negatively, with an average of 56% of those surveyed holding a negative perception of the country.
- The views correspond with the conclusion of the Israel-Lebanon war in 2006; indicating that majority of the international community does not look favourably towards Israel's military posture.

According to a study of the content analysis of UK newspapers to coincide with Israel's 60th anniversary of independence in 1948:

83% of articles on regional peace conveyed the message that Israel did not seek peace.

44% of all articles conveyed the message that Israel was created at the expense of the Palestinians.

27% of all articles conveyed the message that Israel is a successful country.

Content analysis of views about Israel in UK newspaper (in %)

News Articles	Negative	Positive	Neutral
The Guardian	66	7	27
The Independent	55	9	36
BBC Website	43	5	52
All UK Newspapers	36	21	43

Israel has been subjected to several critical resolutions by the United Nations.

8. LOSS OF TOURISM

Tourists in Millions, 1995-2005

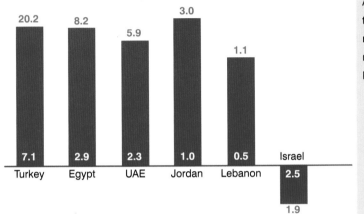

Average rate of cumulative growth of tourism over the decade for Israel's neighbouring countries was 270%, not considering Saudi Arabia which hosts Haj pilgrims.

☐ 1995
▨ 2005

	Turkey	Egypt	UAE	Jordan	Lebanon	Israel
1995	7.1	2.9	2.3	1.0	0.5	
2005	20.2	8.2	5.9	3.0	1.1	

Tourists in Israel

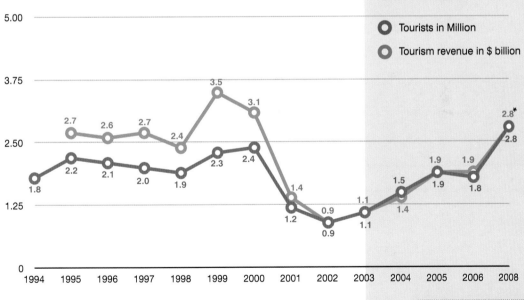

⬤ Tourists in Million
⬤ Tourism revenue in $ billion

*Estimates

Cost of Conflict in the Middle East

Opportunity Loss in Tourism (in $ billions)

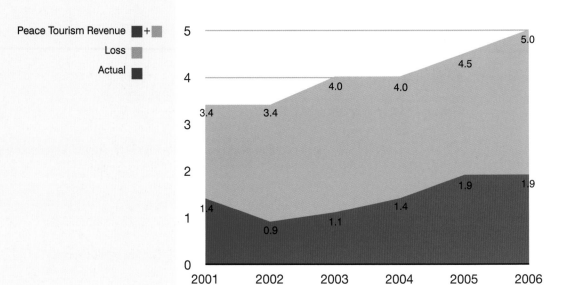

Peace Tourism Revenue ▪ + ▪
Loss ▪
Actual ▪

Since the beginning of Intifada II, Israel suffered tourism revenue loss of over $15 billion during 2001-2006. It was on the path of recovery in 2006. Its tourism increased by 22% in the first half of 2006. However, the war with Hezbollah had a toll with tourism decreasing by 27% in the second half of 2006.

Israeli tourism recovered for the first time in 2008, slightly over the level of 2000. However, in the absence of setback suffered in the first half of the decade, tourist inflow would have been at least 5 million.

9. EMIGRATION

The following news item appeared in several Israeli and international newspapers in April 2007. It is self-explanatory.

Emigration from Israel exceeds immigration, report

Tel Aviv (dpa) - In Israel, the number of emigrants exceeded the number of immigrants for the first time in 20 years, the Israeli daily Yediot Ahronot reported Friday.

Many emigrants were recent arrivals who wanted to leave Israel again, the report said. In 2007, 14,400 immigrants are expected in Israel while 20,000 people are expected to leave the country, according to the report based on figures for the first months of 2007.

The last time emigration exceeded immigration was in the aftermath of the 1973 Yom Kippur War and in 1983 and 1984 when inflation was high.

Meanwhile, the Maariv newspaper reported that approximately a quarter of the Israeli population was considering emigration.

Almost half of the country's young people were thinking of leaving the country, the report said. Their reasons included dissatisfaction with the government, the education system, a lack of confidence in the political ruling class and concern over the security situation.

Cost of Conflict in the Middle East

Several Israeli scholars have attempted to calculate the price of occupying the Palestinian territories.

Comparison of estimates of the Cost of Settlement
1970 & 2005

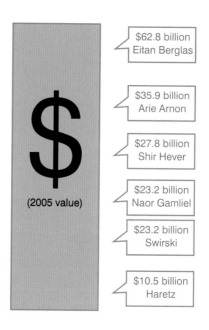

$62.8 billion
Eitan Berglas

$35.9 billion
Arie Arnon

$27.8 billion
Shir Hever

$23.2 billion
Naor Gamliel

$23.2 billion
Swirski

$10.5 billion
Haretz

$
(2005 value)

11. SLUMP IN HOUSE PRICES

Following the second Intifada, there has been a significant drop in housing prices in various parts of the country, as citizens affected by the persistent conflict are unwilling to invest in homes. Certain areas, as shown below are more affected than others, and if the violence in these areas continues prices will continue to drop further, affecting not only the markets but the morale of the people in these areas.

Changes in Average Price of Dwellings (%)

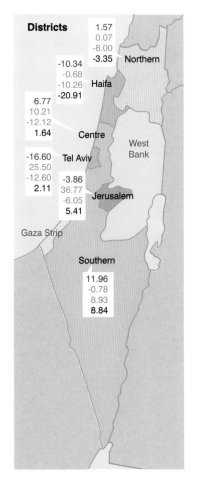

Districts

Northern: 1.57 / 0.07 / -8.00 / -3.35

Haifa: -10.34 / -0.68 / -10.26 / -20.91

Centre: 6.77 / 10.21 / -12.12 / 1.64

Tel Aviv: -16.60 / 25.50 / -12.60 / 2.11

Jerusalem: -3.86 / 36.77 / -6.05 / 5.41

Southern: 11.96 / -0.78 / 8.93 / 8.84

Gaza Strip, West Bank

Israel
-6.47 / 28.09 / -11.60 / -7.52

■ Second Intifada (Q3 2000 - Q2 2003)
▨ (Q2 2003 - Q1 2006)
▨ Israel - Hezbollah War (Q1 - Q4 2006)
■ (Q4 2006 - Q1 2008)

Note: Q refers to quarter

Metropolitan Areas

Gush Dan	Sharon	Qrayot Haifa
-2.24	1.81	6.15
5.22	26.25	-6.26
-5.70	-10.08	-2.81
6.91	-7.41	-12.06

Source : Central Bureau of Statistics

As Israel's economic centre and the location of most foreign embassies, Tel Aviv's housing market suffers the most whenever the country is in conflict. The district of Haifa in northern Israel, which shares a border with Hezbollah-controlled districts in southern Lebanon, was heavily damaged by rocket attacks during the 2006 conflict. The house prices in the district obviously fell. While property prices in other districts have partially recovered since the cessation of conflict at the end of 2006, house prices in Haifa district have continued to fall.

Cost of Conflict in the Middle East

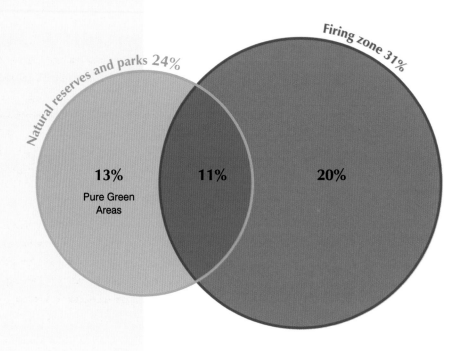

Chapter 7 : Benefits of Warm Peace

INTRODUCTION

We must make a distinction between Warm Peace and Cold Peace. The current peace treaty between Israel and Egypt is an example of Cold Peace, whereby the states have committed to non-aggressive conduct of bilateral relations but there is societal hostility, mistrust and lack of active economic discourse. Cold Peace cannot produce much benefit – even though there may be reduction in defence expenditure and infusion of foreign aid. Israel's military expenditure has declined from 30.3% of GDP in 1975 to about 8% this decade. Nevertheless, in order to reap benefits of conflict settlement, it is necessary to construct a vision of warm peace, which may be defined as not merely absence of violence but also active economic, social, cultural and political harmony.

The success of the Oslo Accord did not last long because the Palestinians did not realise any concrete benefits from it, leading them to desperation by 2000 that further led them to the Second Intifada. The architects of the Oslo Accords had the vision of a warm peace reflected in their discussion on several areas of economic and technical cooperation. The failure was in the absence of implanting good intentions. Any future conflict settlement must be transformed into conflict resolution by emphasis on warm peace strategies.

If comprehensive and warm peace prevails in the Middle East, a number of projects would be feasible that can enhance income, generate employment, create trading opportunities, expand the middle classes and further contribute to peace and stability. Thus, these projects can set in motion a virtuous cycle.

Several cooperative projects have been conceived despite the atmosphere of violence and distrust. They have not been implemented. Many of these projects are in the transport sector. They can not only produce economic benefits but also connect people who have been divided for over six decades. Such linkages can remove the deficit of trust, forge social alliances and foster friendship in the region.

Considering that the current context is that of conflict, only a few projects have been conceptualized and debated which are mentioned here. Once the region ushers in an era of peace, several more projects will be conceived and born, and create a multiplier impact. However, even a few examples which are discussed in public domain demonstrate unlimited scope of benefits from peace.

Cost of Conflict in the Middle East

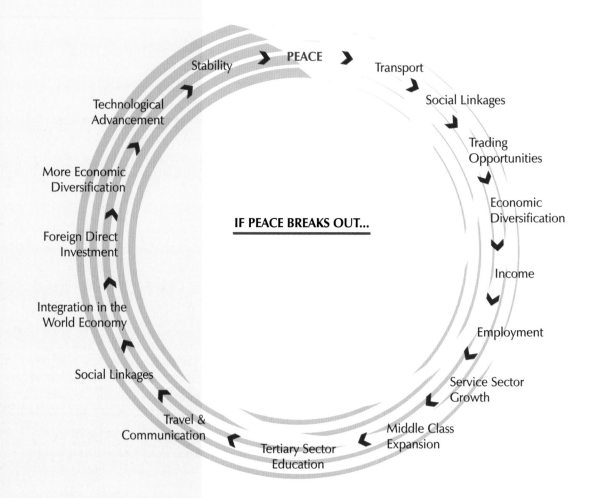

Stability → **PEACE** → Transport

Technological Advancement

Social Linkages

More Economic Diversification

Trading Opportunities

IF PEACE BREAKS OUT...

Foreign Direct Investment

Economic Diversification

Integration in the World Economy

Income

Employment

Social Linkages

Service Sector Growth

Travel & Communication

Middle Class Expansion

Tertiary Sector Education

1. ISRAEL'S PEACE DIVIDEND

Israel's Peace Dividend (PD) can be calculated as follows :

PD = Marginal Increase in GDP − Cost of Change

Where Cost of Change = indemnity to Israeli settlers + compensation to Palestinian refugees + interest;

Marginal Increase in GDP = Peace GDP − Projected GDP considering GDP for 2010 as the basis.

Israel's cost of change = 12.5 + 22.5 + 10.5 = $ 45.5 billion

Annualised payment @ $9.1 billion

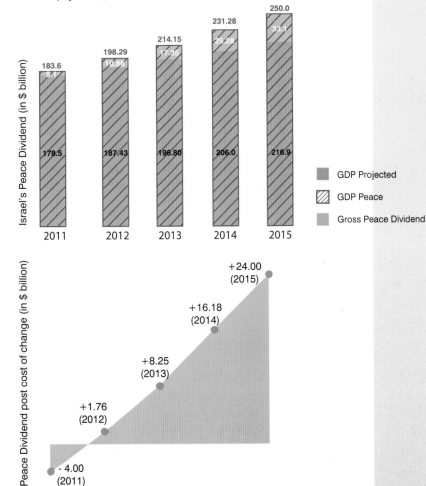

Thus, Peace Dividend per Israeli household will be $4429 per year for the first five years on the basis of the projected population size of 7.3 million at the beginning of the next decade. If peace is maintained along with sound economic policies, Israel can expect to increase its per capita income by more than $5000 per year forever. It's only the first year that the Israeli economy will suffer a net loss. However, it breaks even in the second year of peace and then gains at a fast rate in the years to follow.

Cost of Conflict in the Middle East

Technical Notes

Marginal increase in GDP

This can happen on account of lifting of Arab boycott + increase in trade ($ 5 billion) + increase in tourism ($2 billion) + construction contracts in the Palestinian infrastructure ($1 billion) + marketing and banking opportunities in Dubai for diamond trade and industries + savings in additional military expenditure focussed on the Palestinian targets and items such as wall ($1 billion) + diversion of human capital to productive economy + shift from high alert to training period of reserves + diversion of leadership energy and mindset to growth opportunities + miscellaneous.

Indemnity to Israeli settlers

There are 250,000-300,000 settlers in West Bank, depending on the source of information. In reality, some settlers in the adjoining areas to the Green Line will not need to be settled as a result of 'swap' of lands. Thus, indemnity may apply to maximum 175,000 settlers. Since an average Jewish family has 3.5 members, there will be 50,000 families to be indemnified.

Compensation for Gaza settlers @ US$ 250,000 per family of settlers used as the basis.

West Bank settlers to be indemnified	175,000
Families	50,000
Indemnity	$12.5 billion

Israel does not take into account East Jerusalem in its settler statistics. However, the Palestinian Authority includes East Jerusalem in its calculations. Any sustainable settlement will include a plan for peaceful economic co-existence and cooperation between Jews and Palestinians of East Jerusalem – whatever the nature of the political settlement. Therefore, physical transfer of Jewish families in Jerusalem is not for the purpose of indemnity.

Compensation to Palestinian refugees

The Aix Group has estimated costs of compensation to the Palestinian refugees if there is a resolution of the conflict under the following heads: direct resettlement outlays, property claims, rehabilitation and refugee status compensation. The total is estimated to be in the range of $55-85 billion. However, the group expects Israel to pay only for property claims and international community – particularly including the Arab states – to pay for the rest. Israel's liability is estimated at $15-30 billion on account of property claims. Since it's a wide range, we will use median point for the purpose of our calculations.

Therefore, compensation to Palestinian refugees = $22.5 billion

Interest

Israel will have to consider interest cost of $12.5 billion + $22.5 billion = $35 billion

Assuming 10% rate of interest over 5-year repayment on most lenient terms for political reasons, the total interest will be $10.5 billion.

2. ARAB PEACE DIVIDEND

The Arab Peace Dividend (PD) can be calculated as follows :

PD = Marginal Increase in GDP − Cost of Change

Where Cost of Change = compensation to Palestinian refugees + infrastructure costs of the Palestinian state + interest;

Marginal Increase in GDP = Peace GDP − Projected GDP considering actual (expected) GDP for 2010 as the basis.

Cost of change for the Arabs would be 25+ 15 +12 = $52 billion

Annualised payment $10.4 billion

Normally, the costs will be shared by countries benefiting the most from economic cooperation that will follow the peace process. The following formula can be envisaged, though many other formulae are possible.

Saudi Arabia	50%
UAE	10%
Qatar	10%
Kuwait	10%
Egypt	10%
Others	10%

Saudi Arabia may take responsibility for $5.2 billion

Each other partner may take responsibility for $1 billion

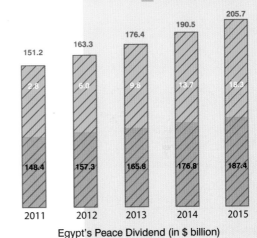

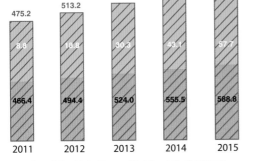

Saudi Arabia's Peace Dividend (in $ billion)

Egypt's Peace Dividend (in $ billion)

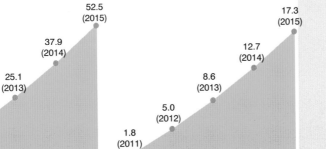

Saudi Arabia's Peace Dividend post cost of change (in $ billion)

Egypt's Peace Dividend post cost of change (in $ billion)

Cost of Conflict in the Middle East

Technical Notes

Marginal increase in GDP

This can happen on account of lifting of Arab boycott + increase in oil exports to Israel ($ 2 billion) + increase in tourism ($2 billion) + savings in defence expenditure + diversion of human capital to productive economy + shift from high alert to training period of reserves + diversion of leadership energy and mindset to growth opportunities + diversification of the economy from oil to other sectors + increase in productive edge of the economy with high-tech cooperation with Israel.

Compensation to the Palestinian refugees

Total costs calculated by Aix Group	$55-85 billion
- Israel's share for property claims	$15-30 billion
= Costs for others	$40-55 billion
Maximum cost for others	$55 billion
- Potential support from G8	$22 billion
- Potential burden for the Arab states	$33 billion

Infrastructure for the Palestinian states

The World Bank/UNDP had estimated Iraq's reconstruction costs at $36 billion. Considering the difference in the situation between Iraq and the Palestinian territories, and also taking into account the reconstruction cost of Kuwait in the 1990s, total infrastructure cost for the Palestinian state would be maximum $ 7 billion including the cost for roads, airport, schools, hospitals and institutions for the West Bank ($6 billion) and reconstruction of Gaza ($1 billion).

Interest

If the expenditure of $40 billion is to be incurred over 5 years, it will carry an interest burden of $12 billion @10%, assuming lenient payment terms are offered for political reasons.

3. PROMISE OF THE SINAI UNDERGROUND WORLD

The Sinai Peninsula brings together Egypt, Palestinian Territories (Gaza), Israel and Jordan.

Joint investments and technology transfer can help develop underground water, oil and gas reserves for the benefit of the region, in the process creating large scale employment for the Egyptian young people.

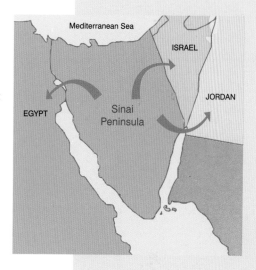

Water

There is 308 billion cubic meters of groundwater in Sinai. At present rate of withdrawal, it can last for more than 400 years. Currently, Egypt depends on Nile, Israel on Galilee and the Palestine Territories on Israel for the supply of water. Joint water development of Sinai for the three countries can enable Sinai and Gaza to grow agriculture and produce a new source of food.

Oil and Gas

Experts have conceived Peace Pipeline from Port Said to Gaza to Israel to Lebanon. Transaction value for Egypt would be about $1-2 billion per year.

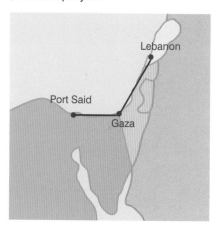

Cost of Conflict in the Middle East

4. RAILWAYS

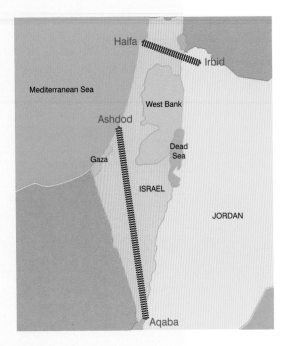

Haifa-Amman Railway Link

- Known as the Hedjaz Railway.
- Also known as the Jezreel Valley Railway in Israel.

1988 - Decision to renew Jezreel Valley Railway

1988 - Survey made

2002 - Israel announces renovation of line from Haifa to Sheikh Hussain Bridge on Jordan River

2008 - Schedule for completion

Europeans are interested in building 2 railway tracks to connect Middle East to Europe; one between Irbid, Jordan and Haifa Israel, and the other linking Aqaba, the Red Sea and the Ashdod port.

Status
As of February 2008, work has not yet started on this line; no official announcement has been made on the freezing or cancellation of the line.

Israel Railways to connect Gaza and Jenin

Israel Railways proposal 2005

Project 1 : Track between Afula and Jenin to link PA and Israel's ports

Project 2 : Track from Erez checkpoint to Gaza, which would be a branch of the Ashkelon-Beersheva line

These links could be connected with routes to Iraq through Jordan and to Egypt through Nitzana.

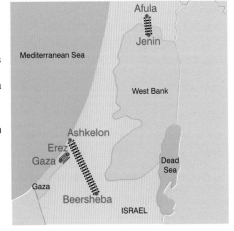

5. GAS DEAL BETWEEN ISRAEL, PALESTINE & BRITISH GAS

◼ BG to drill for natural gas in Gaza Marine field, 36 kilometers off of the Gaza coast to supply to Israel through underwater pipeline.

◼ Pipeline from Gaza Marine field to flow to an Ashkelon refinery.

Estimated time taken for project to get completed : 3 years

Total Deal : $ 4 billion

Benefits to Palestinian Authority : $ 1 billion (Royalties) +
10% of revenue from sale of gas

Total gas availability : 1.4 trillion cubic feet

Estimated per year sale to Israel : 1.5 billion to 1.8 cubic meters
over estimated time period of
10-12 years

Talks began in February 2006

Status : Talks Halted in December 2007

The plan was stayed in December 2007 by BG due to difficulties in negotiating with Israeli government in regards to pricing issues. The Israeli government was also concerned that the revenue might go towards funding Hamas militancy.

Cost of Conflict in the Middle East

6. AQABA PEACE ZONE

The Gulf of Aqaba is a natural transshipment area. Proposals to enhance the area's capacity as a logistic gateway between Asia, Europe and Africa on an international scale and between the Maghreb countries and Persian Gulf on a regional scale, have been presented by the Jordanian, Israeli and Egyptian governments. These proposals include upgrading the Port of Aqaba and road access to it, establishing an "inland port" logistic center connecting transport, manufacturing and storage facilities in the Aqaba-Eilat region, creating international passenger and commercial airports at Aqaba/Ein Evrona and Ras el Naqeb, establishing border and trans-border production zones at Eilat/Aqaba and Ras el Naqeb, and extending rail service between Red and Mediterranean sea ports.

An Agreement on Special Arrangements for Aqaba and Eilat between Israel and Jordan was signed in 1996. This Agreement stipulates that Israel and Jordan will cooperate on issues relating to both towns including: environmental management, pest control; flood management; town zoning and land use policies; energy and natural resources; emergency response services; and the promotion of bi-national and multinational events, such as music festivals, sporting evens, etc. The Agreement also calls for the establishment of a Special Tourism Zone in the region, in which cross border tourism will be encouraged by simplifying crossing procedures, a bi-national Special Economic Zone, and a bi-national Red Sea Marine Peace Park.

Aqaba Eilat Peace Airport

1997	Talks began
>150	Monthly international flights landing at Eilat, Israel
<60	Monthly international flights landing at Aqaba, Jordan
	Issues of disagreement included exact location of new airport and Jordan's intention to use the facility for domestic flights
2006	Talks reopened
	Jordan agreed to have the joint airport service only international carriers.

The benefits of developing a common airport include:

- maximizing use of the Aqaba airport which is under-utilized;

- obviating the need for the current Eilat airport which is operating at near capacity, is environmentally undesirable and is unable to service large aircraft;

- achieving economies of scale by eliminating wasteful duplication of infrastructure and facilities;

- improving air traffic safety in the area;

- exploiting the potential for creating a major logistic center around the airport region;

- enhancing cooperation and developing tourism in the Aqaba-Eilat region.

No Progress 2008

The preferred option is based on an expansion of the existing Aqaba airport which would consist of upgrading the existing runway, constructing new terminals for Israeli-bound traffic and expanding Jordanian terminal facilities. During the first stage, there will be separate terminals for Israeli and Jordanian traffic.

7. PEACE CANAL

This Canal might prevent Dead Sea from drying up.

It may also be used to generate electricity and for the provision of fresh, desalinated water.

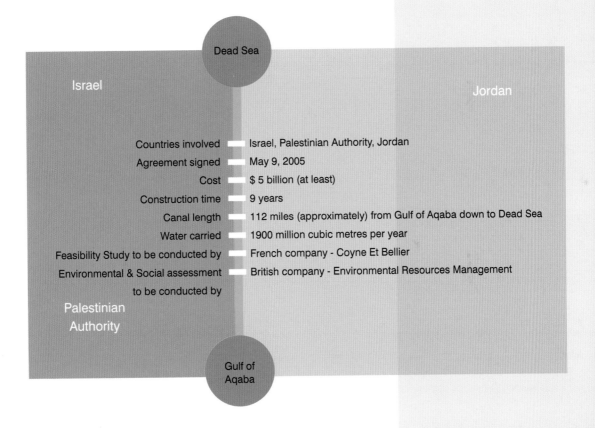

Dead Sea

Israel

Jordan

Countries involved	Israel, Palestinian Authority, Jordan
Agreement signed	May 9, 2005
Cost	$ 5 billion (at least)
Construction time	9 years
Canal length	112 miles (approximately) from Gulf of Aqaba down to Dead Sea
Water carried	1900 million cubic metres per year
Feasibility Study to be conducted by	French company - Coyne Et Bellier
Environmental & Social assessment to be conducted by	British company - Environmental Resources Management

Palestinian
Authority

Gulf of
Aqaba

Cost of Conflict in the Middle East

With the implementation of a peace agreement, Syria would be able to come closer to the Mediterranean Sea for the purpose of trade with the European market.

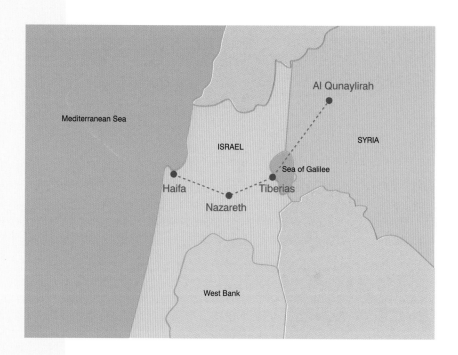

9. JORDAN CONNECTION TO SUEZ CANAL, EGYPT

With a peace agreement in place, Jordan could be linked to the Suez canal through Mizpe Ramon via the Sinai Peninsula, for the purpose of trade.

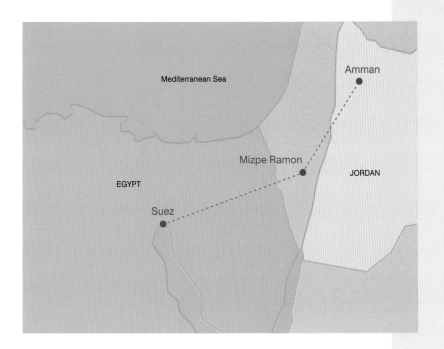

< $2.5 billion
Market Capitalization (2007)

$12 million
Daily turnover (2005) partly affected
by Israel's withdrawal from Gaza

$6 million
Daily turnover (2007) affected by rising
political instability throughout the year

299.4 million
Shares traded (2007)

About 40
Companies listed in 2008

About 40
Companies waiting to be listed

At least another 40
Companies that may be added in peace

Minimum 100
Total companies listed in peace

Minimum $36 million (600% increase)
Daily turnover potential

Minimum $12.5 billion (500% increase)
Market capitalization potential in peace

From 550 in conflict to 2000+ in peace
Al Quds Index potential

The private equity sector is growing in the Gulf region. The Gulf-based private equity private equity investment grew from US$316 million in 2004 to US$5.2 billion in 2006. Some Gulf-based investors expect the amount of capital flowing into local private equity funds to treble in the next five years. There is $2,500 billion of surplus wealth in the GCC countries. The availability of such huge amount of capital creates hope for the growth of the corporate sector, if peace prevails.

11. FMCG SECTOR IN PALESTINE

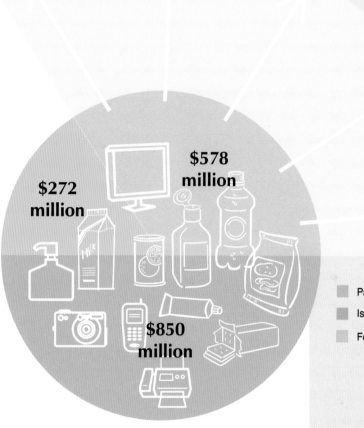

$272 million

$578 million

$850 million

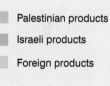

Palestinian products

Israeli products

Foreign products

The market share of Palestinian FMCG companies can grow by 300% from about $600 million in 2008 to $1800 million in times of peace.

- Currently total market size is $1700 million
- Currently there are 40 corporations, which can grow to more than 100
- There is scope for exports to the Gulf states.

Cost of Conflict in the Middle East

The Ben-Gurion International Airport at Tel Aviv could be used by Palestine for its exports and imports to/from Europe and Africa.

This airport might be used to link to the Yaser Arafat International Airport at Gaza.

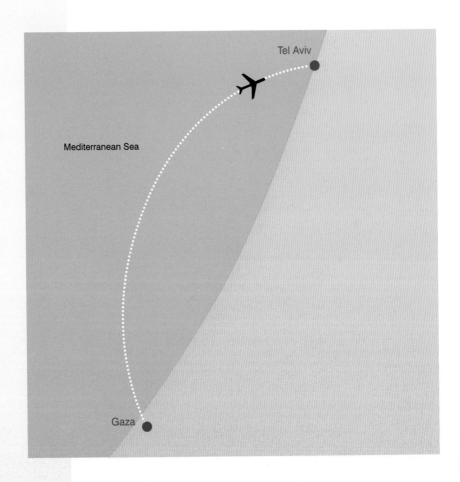

13. INVESTMENT POTENTIAL IN THE PALESTINIAN TERRITORIES

The Palestinian Investment Conference (PIC) was held in Bethlehem, West Bank in May 2008. It raised $1.4 billion and exposed potential for future investments.

1/3rd   1/10th

Projects offered : Construction   High Technology

$650 million

to invest in Wataniya mobile company

$530 million $100 million $65 million $20 million $12 million

invested in :   real estate   industry   information communication technology   insurance   food processing

$350 million

deal signed by Qatari Diar Real Estate Investment Company with a Palestinian partner to build community housing in Ramallah and Nablus

$150 million

UAE's Red Crescent & Authority financing a construction project in Jerusalem

$250 million

Al Ard Al Qabeda (Saudi Arabian Company) has signed a deal to build office towers, malls and a hotel in El Birch (next to Ramallah)

Sectors for investment in future

- **Stone and Marble sector** : contributes 5% to Palestine's GDP; sales reached $270 million in 2005 out of which 32% was domestic, 55% went to Israel and 13% was sold throughout Middle East. It provides 15000 direct jobs in Palestine and accounts for 1.8% of world production. This sector has a fast growing potential of 10%.
- **Agriculture and Food Processing sector** : with potential to process and export fruits, olives, olive oil, strawberries, vegetables and cut flowers.
- **Banking sector** : as presently 21 banks operate in Palestine. Out of these, 10 are Palestinian with total assets of $1.355 billion. The 12 foreign banks include 9 Jordanian, 2 Egyptian and HSBC Middle East with total assets of $ 4.128 billion. In peace time with the growth of industry, construction, trading, and services, the growth of the banking sector is bound to follow.
- **Energy sector** : as the Ministry of Energy and Natural Resources expects the demand for electricity in West Bank and Gaza to grow 4 times in the next 15 years; hence, the Palestinian Energy and Natural Resources Authority (PENRA) is encouraging private sector investment in this sector.

Cost of Conflict in the Middle East

Tourist Potential

- According to the Israeli Ministry of Tourism, 800, 000 of the tourists that came to Israel in 2005 were Christian tourists.
- Such tourists are interested in visiting biblical towns such as Bethlehem and Jericho within Palestinian Authority.

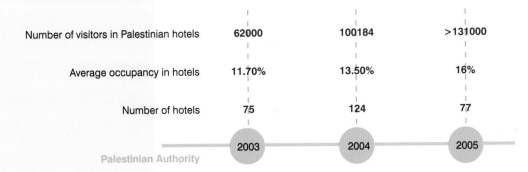

	2003	2004	2005
Number of visitors in Palestinian hotels	62000	100184	>131000
Average occupancy in hotels	11.70%	13.50%	16%
Number of hotels	75	124	77

Palestinian Authority

- If a peace agreement is implemented, a lot more of the Christian tourists that Israel gets every year, would be interested in staying in Palestinian hotels, in Jericho and Bethlehem, instead of returning back to Israel that same day. This would bolster both economies.
- Thus, peace can bring about boom in investments in hotels and ancillary businesses in the tourism sector.

Chapter 8 : Costs to the International Community

INTRODUCTION

The conflict in the Middle East has cost the world economy and humankind in many more ways than is apparent. The conflict in the Middle East is closely intertwined with terrorist attacks on the United State and its allies, the US led War on Terror and the impact of these developments on oil prices. Granted that terrorism and war on terror has its roots in Afghanistan and Pakistan and granted that rise in oil prices is to some extent a function of demand from emerging economies and manipulation by market speculators, the conflict in the Middle East still has a major bearing on these developments. It is not at all suggested that the Middle East is the only driver of terrorism and War on Terror or of oil price movement with 100% weight. However, the conflict in the Middle East would account for at least 30 to 50% of the weight of the total weight of drivers.

The rise in oil prices from 2003 to 2008, through its impact on transportation costs, has effectively nullified the liberalisation of trade since the 1970s. The conflict in the Middle East is responsible for at least half of the weight of this development. Similarly, the conflict plays a role – an immeasurable one – in worsening of the fiscal deficit of the United States, travails of global transport industries, flight ban on several people, and other forms of economic, political and dignity deficits of people around the world.

The cost for the international community is not only to be seen in terms of what is lost by the conflict, resulting oil prices hike, inflation, human casualties, but also in terms of what is neglected. The conflict draws attention away from other global issues such as poverty alleviation, health, migration, and the health of the global financial system. In the absence of the conflict in the Middle East, would the world have a war on terror or a war on poverty? It is still possible that groups such as Al Qaeda may continue acts of terror but they will then face a combined might of all international and regional actors.

Cost of Conflict in the Middle East

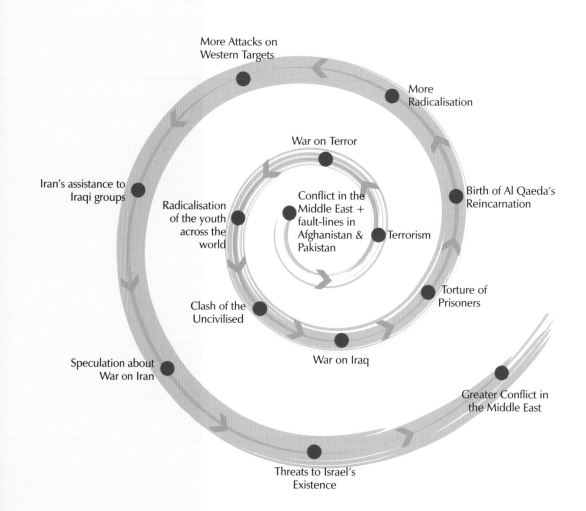

More Attacks on
Western Targets

More
Radicalisation

War on Terror

Iran's assistance to
Iraqi groups

Birth of Al Qaeda's
Reincarnation

Radicalisation
of the youth
across the
world

Conflict in the
Middle East +
fault-lines in
Afghanistan &
Pakistan

Terrorism

Clash of the
Uncivilised

Torture of
Prisoners

Speculation about
War on Iran

War on Iraq

Greater Conflict in
the Middle East

Threats to Israel's
Existence

1. OIL, TARIFFS & YOU

There is a strong correlation between the conflict in the Middle East and rise in oil prices. In the last 50 years, there have been 5 occasions of major leaps in oil prices.

Year of Leap in the Price of Oil

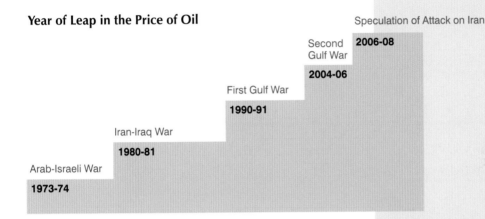

Speculation of Attack on Iran

Second Gulf War **2006-08**

First Gulf War **2004-06**

Iran-Iraq War **1990-91**

Arab-Israeli War **1980-81**

1973-74

On all other occasions during 1959-2009, for a period of half century, oil prices have either stabilised at the previous level or declined. Thus, conflict in the Middle East has proved to be the single most significant driver of oil price leaps.

Oil prices have seen dramatic rise since 2003 and violent oscillations in 2008. While growing demand from China and India and market speculations have played a role in this development, the period of steep rise coincides with a major war in Iraq and speculation about an attack on Iran.

World Crude Oil Prices ($ per Barrel) – December each year

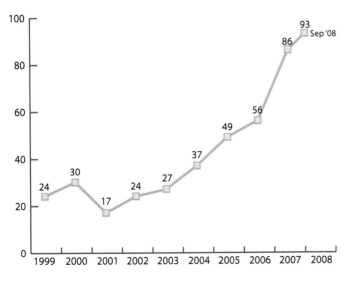

Cost of Conflict in the Middle East

Rise in oil prices influences transportation costs and hinders trade.

Share of fuel cost in the total cost for all forms of transportation

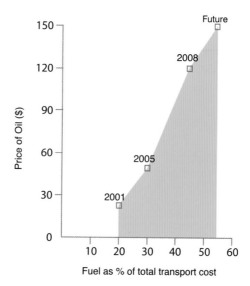

Converting Transportation Costs into Equivalent "Tariff" Rates

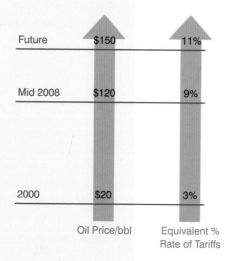

Estimated average tariff for world trade

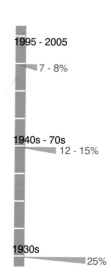

If oil prices hover between $120-150 per barrel, they constitute a burden on the world economy equivalent to 10% tariff – comparable to pre-GATT era. Thus, increase in oil prices nullify significant portion of the progress in trade liberalisation in the last four decades. To the extent, conflict in the Middle East is responsible for oil price hike it is also responsible for negating progress in the liberalisation of world trade since the 1970s.

2. NO FLY LIST

The United States Transportation Security Administration (TSA) maintains a No-Fly List of persons who are not allowed to board a plane as threat to civil aviation security and Terrorist Watch List of persons who are subjected intensive screening at airports. In addition to those on these lists, several thousands of people in the 'false positive' category (coincidence of names, even partially with those on the No-Fly List and Terrorist Watch List) are also caused inconvenience while travelling to, from or within the United States.

No-Fly List

Date	Estimated Number
September 11, 2001	16
December 2001	594
December 2002	1,000
March 2006	44,000
August 2008	100,000

1,000   Al Qaeda core strength in December 2008

100,000   No-Fly List December 2008

1,000,000   Terrorist Watch List December 2008

2,000,000   Terrorist Watch List December 2012

Travel Restrictions since 9/11
- Restrictions (earlier ban) on liquid items in passenger hand-baggage
- Passenger profiling and secondary screening
- Armed law enforcement officers or federal marshals and armed pilots present on flight
- Increased screening of airport employees.

Cost of Conflict in the Middle East

US Appropriations for the Global War On Terror : 2001-2008
(price in $ billions)

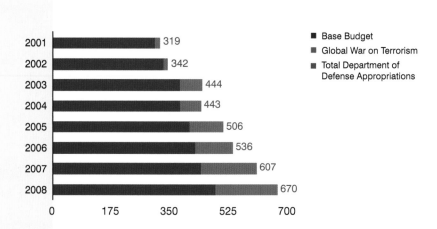

The US Congressional Research Service estimates total US appropriations for the 'global war on terrorism' at $805.1 billion for Fiscal Years 2001-2008.

The bill of War on Terror in the US budget coincides with the budget deficit. The US budget was in surplus until 2001 and then turned into deficit from 2002 to 2008. With growing budget deficit, public debt has also soared. The US deficit and public debt is a combined effect of expenditure on conflicts related to the Middle East and mismanagement of the economy.

US Budget surplus and deficit since 9/11 : 2000-2007

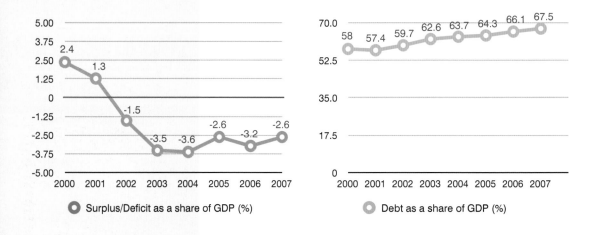

4. UN BILL FOR PEACE-KEEPING

UN Peace Keeping Missions in the Middle East

Mission	UNDOF	UNIFIL	UNTSO
Location	Golan Heights	Southern Lebanon	Middle East
Duration	1974 to present	1978 to present	1948 to present
Overall Personnel	1,249	13,294	393
Fatalities	43	276	49
Approved budget (July 2008-June 2009)	$47.86 million	$680.93 million	$66.22 million

Cost of Conflict in the Middle East

EU assistance to Palestine

€ 3.2 BILLION

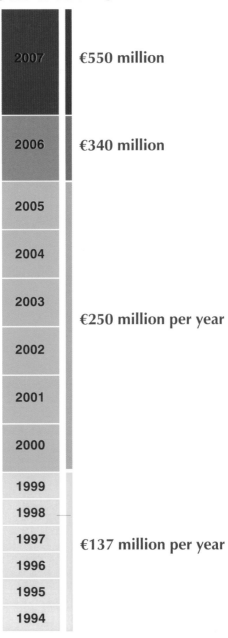

2007	€550 million
2006	€340 million
2005	
2004	
2003	€250 million per year
2002	
2001	
2000	
1999	
1998	
1997	€137 million per year
1996	
1995	
1994	

6. SPREAD OF AL QAEDA

Al Qaeda has its origins in the US support for insurgency in Afghanistan in the 1980s against the Soviet occupation, the training of Taliban in Pakistan, the First Gulf War, the continuing deadlock on the Palestinian issue, and the radicalisation of youth in the Arab countries. Al Qaeda I (the new incarnation of Al Qaeda with a base in Iraq) has its origins in the Iraq War.

Thus, Al Qaeda is a combined result of the US policies in the Middle East and Afghanistan and political and economic fault-lines in those countries.

Senator Obama, in his acceptance speech for the presidency of the United States in September 2008, said that Al Qaeda had spread to 80 countries by 2008.

1,000 + 3,000 + 5,000 = 9,000

| people killed from several countries in attacks by Al Qaeda or its affiliates in Algiers, Amman, Istanbul, London, Madrid, Riyadh, Tunis, and other places in the first decade of the 21st century | people killed in the Al Qaeda attack on the World Trade Centre on 9/11, 2001 | coalition troops killed in Afghanistan and Iraq from 2003 to 2008 | human cost of the Middle East conflict for the international community during 2001-2008 |

Cost of Conflict in the Middle East

7. THE RETURN OF TALIBAN

The attack on World Trade Centre was a joint project of certain elements in Afghanistan and Pakistan. However, the obsession with the Middle East, and the consequent attack on Iraq, has resulted in the neglect of the international community's strategic objectives in Afghanistan-Pakistan and the return of Taliban in southern and eastern parts of Afghanistan.

Coalition Troops 2008

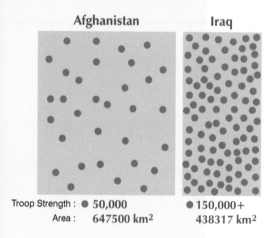

Afghanistan — Iraq

Troop Strength :	● 50,000	● 150,000+
Area :	647500 km²	438317 km²

Coalition Military Fatalities in Afghanistan

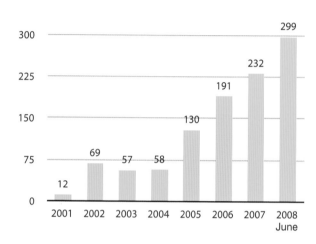

Suicide Bomb Attacks in Afghanistan

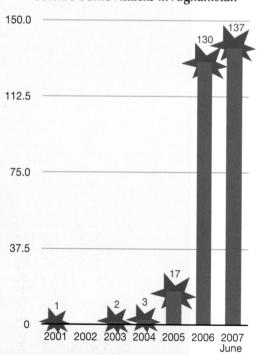

Opium Poppy Cultivation in Afghanistan (in hectares)

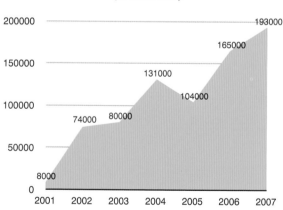

Poppy Cultivation has been on a steady rise in Afghanistan since 2001. The crops are generally grown in the areas where the Taliban are prevalent (mainly in the South). Poppy cultivation is reported to have reduced to 157,000 hectares in August 2008 - due to drought conditions in areas of cultivation.

8. ASCENT OF AYATOLLAHS

The US obsession with the Middle East – attack on Iraq, neglecting Afghanistan – has caused ascent of Ayatollahs and President Ahmedinejad in Iran.

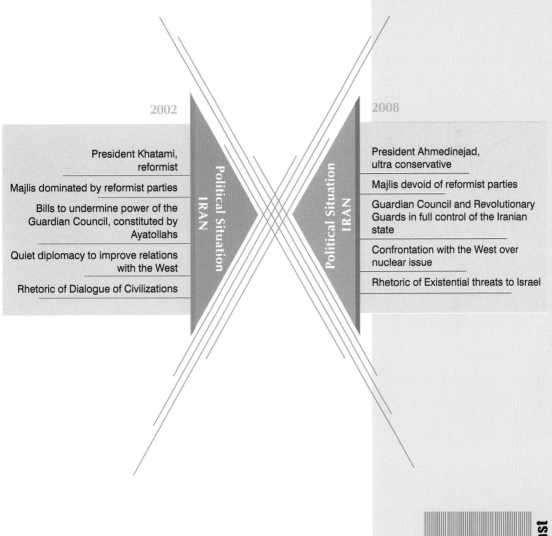

2002

Political Situation
IRAN

President Khatami,
reformist

Majlis dominated by reformist parties

Bills to undermine power of the
Guardian Council, constituted by
Ayatollahs

Quiet diplomacy to improve relations
with the West

Rhetoric of Dialogue of Civilizations

2008

Political Situation
IRAN

President Ahmedinejad,
ultra conservative

Majlis devoid of reformist parties

Guardian Council and Revolutionary
Guards in full control of the Iranian
state

Confrontation with the West over
nuclear issue

Rhetoric of Existential threats to Israel

Cost of Conflict in the Middle East

Iran's Political Allies in Iraq, Palestine and Lebanon
Seats in Parliament

Iraq

2000	2008
Nil	53/275

Moqtada supporters & SCIRI

Lebanon

2000	2008
8/128	14/128

Hezbollah

Palestine

1996	2008
0/88	74/132

Hamas

Annual Arab Public Opinion Survey, conducted in Sunni countries, in 2008 revealed the following:

67%   Believe that Iran has a right to its nuclear programme

46%   Believe that Iran's nuclear research is peaceful

44%   Believe that Iran should develop nuclear weapons

The same survey reveals that the top three leaders in the Sunni Arab countries are the leaders close to Iran's Ayatollahs, in the following order, in 2006 and again in 2008:

- Hassan Nasrallah, Leader of Hezbollah
- Bashar Assad, President of Syria
- Mohammed Ahmedinejad, President of Iran

9. LOSS OF AMERICAN CREDIBILITY

Several public opinion polls conducted by American institutions indicate that the United States has lost its moral leadership because of its policies on the Middle East. This is particularly true of the public opinion in the Arab countries but not limited to them.

Annual Arab Public Opinion Poll, 2008 (in Arab countries)

88% United States is the biggest threat to world peace

83% Overall unfavourable view of the United States

75% Believe that the US policy is guided by objectives of dominance and oil control

70% No confidence in the United States

65% No trust in US democracy promotion

Globe Scan Survey publicised by BBC World Service, 2007 (covering 25 countries across the world)

73% Disapprove US actions in Iraq

68% Believe that the United States is a creator of conflicts

60% Disapprove US handling of the Iran nuclear issue

52% Believe that influence of the United States is a negative factor in the world

Cost of Conflict in the Middle East

10. CREDIBILITY OF INTERNATIONAL INSTITUTIONS

After the success of the Madrid and Oslo processes in the early 1990s, the failure of various peace processes has damaged the credibility of the international institutions. There are no opinion polls available to examine this. Out of the 7 major peace initiatives during 2000-2008, all have failed. During the same period 5 major violent conflicts took place: (1) Second Intifada (2) Iraq War (3) Israel-Hezbollah Missile War (4) Fatah-Hamas conflict (5) Iran-Israel/US Cold War. Also, increasing dependence on violence by all parties without referring to the international institutions.

Process	Sponsor	Year	Outcome
Camp David Talks between Israel-PLO	United States	2000	X
Clinton Plan for Israel-Syria	United States	2000	X
Arab Peace Plan	Saudi Arabia, Arab League	2002	X
Road Map	Quartet	2003	X
Mecca Accord between Fatah and Hamas	Saudi Arabia	2007	X
Arab Peace Plan (revised)	Saudi Arabia, Arab League	2007	X
Annapolis Process	US Government	2007	X

Credibility of International Institutions : SFG score

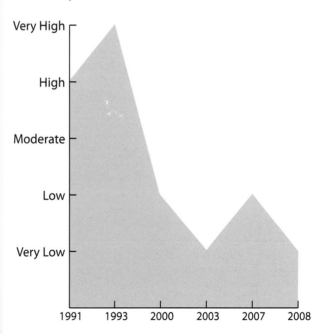

11. FUTURE RISK: INTERNATIONAL ECONOMIC WARFARE

There are already indications of Iran preparing for an economic warfare with the United States, with some assistance from Russia.

June 2006
_____
Establishment of Russian Oil Bourse

December 2007
_____
Iran's shift of oil trade to non-dollar currencies

February 2008
_____
Establishment of Iranian Oil Bourse

Future Risk

Cause	Effect
• If US dollar falls to Euro 1 = $2 or thereabouts • If Iran and Russia enforce all oil contracts in non-dollar currencies, covering 10% of oil market • If Venezuela shifts sizable portion of its market from the US to China • If China switches part of its reserves and trade to non-dollar currencies	• Loss of confidence in the US dollar as a reserve currency, and its swift depreciation • Rush among Chinese, Russian and Arab investors to buy US assets • Stiff investment protection legislation by the United States • Counter-measures for investment protection by US economic partners • Unpredictable movements in capital • Collapse of banks • Collapse of markets for all assets • Worldwide recession • Political fall-out

Risk

High - if there is polarisation over the Middle East conflict between (a) United States, Israel and Arab governments (b) Iran, Russia and Arab population, with China supporting the (b) group from outside

Moderate – if there is growing confrontation between Iran and the United States/Israel but Russia is neutral

Nil – if there is rapprochement between the United States and Iran or if the Israel-Palestinian conflict is being solved and therefore all major powers develop stakes in global stability.

Cost of Conflict in the Middle East

If there is a major war involving Iran, there is a high risk of Iran closing the Strait of Hormuz by placing landmines and sinking ships. If this happens, the strait will remain closed for over two months, as cleaning the strait and resuming operations for business would take an estimated 40-60 days.

Total oil Exports in the world = 46 million barrels per day
Oil carried through the Strait of Hormuz = 16-20 million barrels per day = about 40 % of the worlds globally traded oil

90% of Oil exported by 6 countries travels through the Strait of Hormuz.

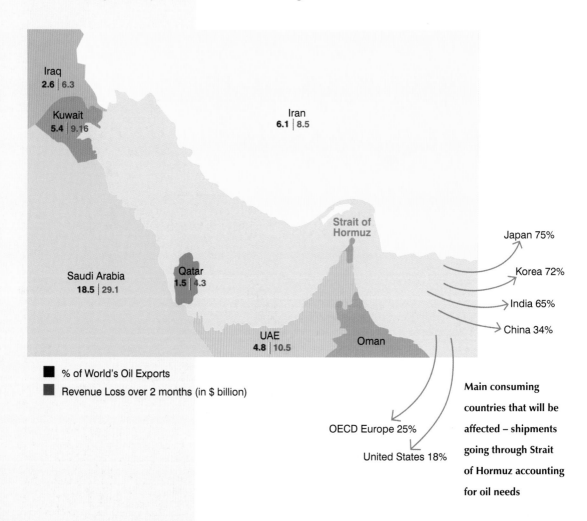

Chapter 9 : Scenarios 2025

Global Economy : Post Hydrocarbon

Two-State Solution

Global Politics : Unipolar

Regional Confrontation

Where Suspicion Prevails

Where People Smile

Where Brutality Reigns

Where Equations Change

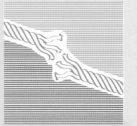

Global Politics : Multi-polar

Regional Cooperation

One-State Solution

Global Economy : Oil

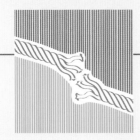

This scenario occurs in a world where the United States still retains it dominant position while the world economy gradually moves from heavy oil dependence to a mixed post-hydrocarbon economy. The United States and its allies have a strategic interest in the Middle East, but the economic interest of the international community in the Middle East is declining. The world is simply fed up with continuing violence and they want a quick solution, even a provisional and fragile one.

In this scenario, the international community forces Israel to accept a provisional two-state solution and the Arab states to guarantee Israel's security and end their economic boycott against Israel. Israel vacates the West Bank with minor exchange of territories with the Palestinian Authority for practical and security reasons. There are commissions to look into questions such as the Status of Jerusalem and compensation for the Palestinian refugees, which are involved in endless discussions.

The fragile truce reduces the level of violence but it does not remove tension from the region. All countries find the need to be in a state of military preparedness. The arms race continues. Iran, in particular, is suspected of having successfully developed nuclear weapons. Iran enjoys support from some Arab states and political groups. Some Arab states explore developing nuclear weapons. The Arab world remains divided with Syria firmly in the Iranian camp. Lebanon and Iraq face internal turmoil due to violent sectarian conflicts between groups supporting Iran and secular Arabs respectively.

With leaders in all countries occupied with security issues and Arab business leaders refusing to trade with Israel in practice, despite ending the boycott in theory, there is no substantial change in the economic situation. Most economies grow at 3-6% per year. There is no significant diversification of oil economies. The share of the region in technological developments is marginal. There is a slight improvement in the condition of children. In the Palestinian territories, they are no longer stopped at check-points on the way to schools. However, investment in education is insignificant. Bright young people migrate overseas. There is a general sense of despair.

Despair leads to discontent among young people since peace has not delivered any concrete gains. The support for political groups and states with extremist views continues to oscillate, increasing and decreasing from time to time. Hamas becomes weak and a more absolutist group, Islamic Jihad, gains popularity not only among the Palestinians but also among population at large across the region. Fatah is a minor player. The Islamic Jihad aims to stir unrest in Jordan and Lebanon with an aim to install Islamic regimes in both the countries. Israel elects most of its cabinet, and not merely the Prime Minister, from persons with a military background.

The international community keeps pressure on all sides for the situation not to slide into a war. There is no peace and no war.

WHERE BRUTALITY REIGNS

This scenario occurs in a world where the United States retains it dominant position and the world economy heavily depends on oil and natural gas from the Middle East. There is no breakthrough in any new form of energy. The fast industrializing countries in Asia and Latin America compete for hydrocarbon resources in Asia and Africa. Europe is constantly involved in a see-saw game with the Russian Federation. The United States dictates terms in the Middle East, with little opposition from its partners and competitors.

The Palestinian groups refuse to accept any temporary solution, or rescind it after a few years of experimentation. Fatah disappears in oblivion. Hamas and Islamic Jihad are weakened with a new group supported by Iran gaining popularity in the Palestinian territories. Frustrated by the absence of a pliable dialogue partner on the Palestinian side, Israel continues or resumes settlements in the West Bank and consolidates its position in East Jerusalem. It creates a regime comparable to the South African Apartheid in the 20th century. It resorts to housing demolitions, arrests and barriers on a large scale – unimaginable at the beginning of the 21st century. The Palestinian groups resort to suicide bombings and missile attacks with high frequency. Both sides particularly concentrate their attacks on targets popular with young people such as schools, colleges, cinema houses and cafes.

Iran tests nuclear weapons and ICBMs despite worldwide condemnation. However, Russia and China block the UN Security Council from any punitive action against Iran beyond verbal criticism. Some Arab states explore developing nuclear weapons. All countries in the region are in a heightened state of military preparedness. There is a full-blown arms race with the United States and its allies arming Israel and selected Gulf States, while Russia and China arm Iran and its camp followers.

The governments in the region ignore the economy. Growth rates slide to zero or negative. Defence expenditure in almost every country crosses 15% of GDP. There is marginal investment in health. Governments withdraw funds from education, leaving it to the private sector. In the Palestinian territories, schools are closed for most of the year. In Israel, Jordan and Egypt, pupils have to study with security forces guarding the schools buildings. There is increase in unemployment, which further provides large scale recruitment for extremist groups. The regional extremist groups target the regimes in Jordan and Egypt and eventually succeed in dethroning them. Lebanon and Iraq are also destabilised. Extremist Sunni regimes in Jordan and Egypt enter into a simultaneous cooperative and competitive relationship with extremist Shia regimes in Iraq and Lebanon. There is internal polarisation and frequent outbreak of sectarian violence in Iraq and Lebanon. The Kurds in Iraq take advantage of the situation to try to carve out a state of their own. Other regimes open to conciliation with Israel change their stance and fuel anti-Israeli sentiment. A vicious cycle is set in where Israel consolidates its hold over the West Bank, breaking off Gaza from all transport and communication links with outside world.

It is a matter of time before a massive war takes place between Iran and Israel, along with civil wars across the region.

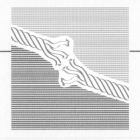

This scenario occurs in a world where there is no single superpower. The United States has declined in its importance due to its consistent mismanagement of economy over two decades – as a result of the preference of its leaders to support privileged interest groups and venture into overseas wars from time to time. The world economy still depends on oil. Russia re-emerges as a major power with the Europeans adapting an ambivalent attitude towards it, thanks to their dependence on Russian oil and gas. China has also emerged as an important player. Iran has undergone either a behavioural or regime change and emerged as an important player with its oligopoly over natural gas and a modernizing economy. Europe, Turkey, India and Japan also have an increased say in global governance.

Israeli leaders fail to conclude a two-State agreement to the satisfaction of the Palestinian people. The Palestinian groups with strong support from Iran and Arab states change their strategy. They give up their demand for two-State solution after the failure of one final round of negotiations and demand a one-state democratic state where they have a majority. The United States is not in a position to support Israel countered by Russia and China. The Europeans also give up all hope for a two-State solution and support one-State arrangement provided it is democratic and respectful of human rights. The extremist Palestinian groups give up acts of violence and join the democratic mainstream. There is a period of struggle between Palestinian and Jewish political parties. Finally, the international community forces a power-sharing constitutional agreement whereby the Head of State is Jewish, but the Head of Government is a Palestinian and the cabinet is divided. Alternatively, the top slots are shared on a revolving basis. The constitution provides for power-sharing in the cabinet as well as in the Parliament.

The Israeli population loses its privileged position in housing, jobs and utilities. The population in the unified state is almost 20 million in 2025 with the Jewish component accounting for 40%, Muslims 58% and a small minority of Christians and others. Many Jewish families migrate abroad. Some accept reconciliation and forge partnerships with the Palestinians, using their own superior technical strengths and networks around the world. The Arabs lift the economic boycott and invite Israeli business companies to facilitate economic exchange. There is a mixed response from the Israeli business community. Economic growth rates are around 5-6% in most countries. There is a debate in the education sector. One stream of thought emphasises plurality and scientific outlook, while another stream promotes religious orthodoxy.

With the new unified state, some groups try to bring about regime change in Egypt and Jordan through non-violent means. There are sectarian tensions in the region but are confined to localised fights and riots. There is no support for escalating the sectarian strife to a wider level.

With stability in the Israel-Palestinian State and transformation of Iran, the key challenge for the Middle East now is the management of plural societies in Iraq, Lebanon and Syria.

WHERE PEOPLE SMILE

This scenario occurs in a world where a multi-polar global order makes it impossible for any one country to emerge as a superpower. The United States accepts its reduced role in global politics and concentrates on domestic prosperity and technological leadership. Russia, China, Japan, Europe, Iran, India, Turkey, South Africa, Brazil and many other countries have stakes in global decision-making processes. The world economy shifts from its overdependence on oil and natural gas to solar, tidal, wind, geothermal and other forms of energy. There are major technological breakthroughs in renewable energy and clean technologies.

In this scenario, the international community does not simply want to accept a violent conflict in a region in which the world has fewer stakes. The Israeli and Palestinian leaders foresee that either side cannot count on external support and move towards reconciliation based on two states as per the 1967 borders, special access to Jerusalem for all religious groups and a negotiating process for addressing the refugee problem, as well as confidence building measures to preserve peace.

With the resolution of the Israel-Palestinian conflict, the collective Arab leadership is now focussed on stability in Iraq and Lebanon. The Arab League acquires new strength. It is tasked by member states to work on creative conflict resolution mechanisms within and between countries. Saudi Arabia and Iran form a joint council to contain potential sectarian strife in the region.

There is a noticeable decline in tension in the region. Most countries bring their defence expenditure down to around 3-4% of GDP. They use the peace dividend to set up training facilities for civilian industries to transfer young people from the security sector to industry and services. There is heavy investment in modern education. The region collaborates across boundaries, religions and sects to claim global leadership in knowledge creation driven by plurality, freedom of critical enquiry and scientific pursuit.

The Arab business leaders lift the boycott of Israel and send delegations to discuss concrete projects, blending Israeli technical expertise with surpluses generated over the years. They build new railway lines, canals, environmental parks, industries, and financial companies through Arab-Israeli joint ventures. The stock markets in the region soar. Business leaders are keen on investing in technological breakthroughs to push the post-hydrocarbon revolution, solve water problems and promote tourism. Most countries have growth rates of 7 to 9% on a consistent basis.

There is a movement towards democratisation with political groups capable of delivering social and economic goods winning elections. It is essential to have strong management or intellectual credentials to be able to move to the top of political parties and governments. There is a demand for free movement of capital and labour across the region. With a gradual beginning in 2025, the region hopes to create the Middle East Economic Union by 2050 and also to play a greater role in the community of nations.

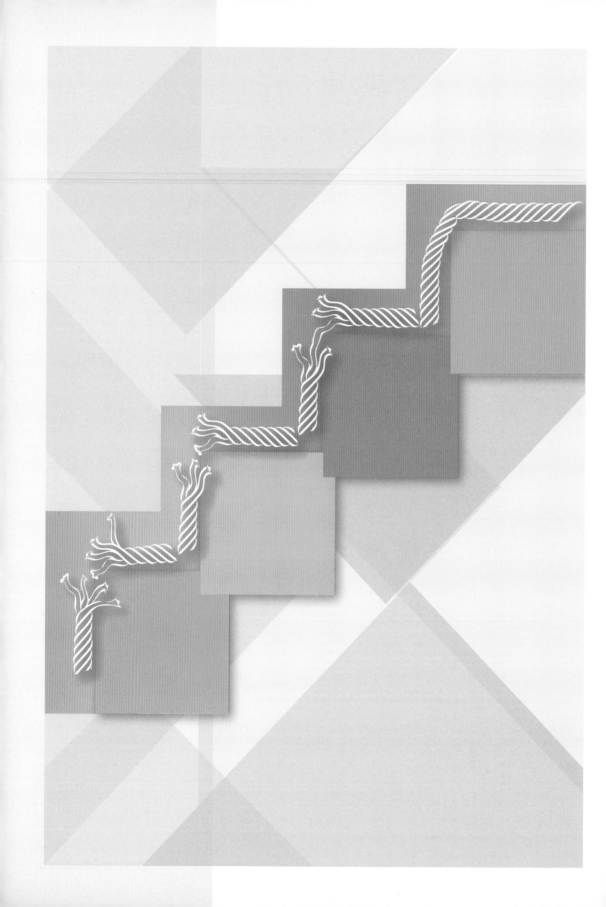

Chapter 10 : Peace Building Ladder

This chapter contemplates a process to make the last scenario in the earlier chapter, Where People Smile, a feasible one.

Stage 1 – United States revises its interests in the Middle East

- In early 2009, the new President is presented with recommendations by the National Intelligence Council in its 4 year report, to reduce America's dependence on the Middle East for oil within 8-10 years.

- With the new energy vision, Washington discovers that a lasting peace in the Middle East would be in their interest.

- The new President of the United States commits to withdrawing troops from Iraq by agreement with the Government of Iraq, within a fixed time-frame and, in a phased manner.

- The US approaches friendly nations in Western Europe to initiate a Middle East dialogue, similar to the Madrid process.

Stage 2 – Confidence Building Measures

- European mediators decide that at first a quiet conversation needs to be initiated with leaders, where certain Confidence Building Measures would help generate some goodwill, and address immediate security concerns.

- Israel adopts a more humane approach towards the people of Gaza and the West Bank, ending the blockades and barriers, and freezing settlements.

- Israel hands over to Lebanon detailed maps of the areas its forces had targeted with cluster bombs, to enable them to be rendered safe. International agencies applaud the move.

- All Palestine groups reciprocate with a ceasefire, and stop all acts of violence against Israeli people.

- The Mecca Agreement is revived, leading to a national unity government between major political factions representing the Palestinian people.

Cost of Conflict in the Middle East

- Talks begin between Sunni and Shia leaders of the region, jointly sponsored by Saudi Arabia and Iran, to reduce the deficit of trust within the Islamic world.

- Travel restrictions are reduced between nations, along with lifting of bans on discussion with parties considered 'enemies' or 'outsiders'. Arab League partially lifts the boycott to allow direct interface between politicians, diplomats and government officials.

- There are several visits by senior diplomats, leaders, and personalities from Israel to all Arab countries and vice versa.

- Arab governments informally ask their media leaders to tone down Arab rhetoric hostile to Jews as a people, to Judaism as a religion and to Israel as a state. Israeli and Jewish antagonism towards Arabs and Muslims is less evident.

- The leader of the Shi'ite Amal party, an ally of Syria and Hizbollah, reiterates his October 2006 statement that "now is the time to return to peace negotiations with Israel".

- All efforts made by other organizations involved in bridge building initiatives between societies are recognized.

- Iraqi factions agree to sit down and draw up conclusive plans to unite the country.

- Israel announces that as long as violence is not directed against it, construction of the "security barrier" in the West Bank would be frozen and the checkpoints and roadblocks steadily reduced.

- Israel releases 500 prisoners "without blood on their hands", including Hamas lawmakers and mayors.

- Hamas releases Israeli soldiers in its jurisdiction, and urges other groups to do the same.

- Involved European diplomats hail the commitments made as historical and urge the nations to follow through on them.

Stage 3 – Talks for Talks

- European mediators meet all parties – including representatives of governments and major elected groups – to gather their perspectives on the definition of key issues.

- The mediators seek consensus on proposed participants including – 1. States from the region; 2. Groups introducing electoral mandate; 3. External powers with demonstrated stakes in the region. They may not include Iran at this stage and leave this issue for a semi-permanent conference to determine at a later stage.

- The mediators prepare an agenda for a launch summit and a semi-permanent conference.

- The mediators prepare a structure of working groups and committees.

- The mediators seek agreement of all parties on pre-negotiation principles and rules of procedure.

Stage 4 – Middle East Summit

- Recognizing the need to take the process forward to detail concrete steps, a Middle East Summit is convened by the United Nations and co-sponsored by the Quartet.

- The summit is attended by Saudi Arabia, Israel, all border nations, non-state actors, and other world leaders.

- A formal decision is made to end the Arab Boycott.

- In the wider region, Morocco, Tunisia, Oman, Bahrain and the UAE declare their intentions in principle to upgrade their future relations with the Israeli state.

- Algeria, Kuwait, Yemen and Libya follow suit, provided the current moves are irreversible and lead to a permanent peace with full withdrawal, apart from equitable land swaps.

- The leaders at the summit agree to discuss the Palestinian refugee problem at a later stage.

- Donors announce support to repair the Yasser Arafat International Airport in Gaza, support for a seaport, and an agro-industrial park in the West Bank as part of a 'corridor for peace and prosperity'.

- G-8 announces plans for a pledging conference to revive trade, tourism and other forms of development with countries in the region.

- The Jordanian, Palestinian and Israeli Governments renew consultations about creating the Peace Canal.

- The EU-funded 'Israeli-Palestinian NGOs Forum' devises a strategy to engage both civil societies in the push for peace and reconciliation at the grass-roots level.

- Israel releases most of the remaining 10,000 Palestinian political prisoners.

- A formal resolution is passed creating an inclusive semi-permanent conference to work out the details of all decisions taken.

Stage 5 – Inclusive Semi-Permanent Conference

- This conference will discuss final, comprehensive and sustainable solutions to all those conflicts in the Middle East agreed in Stage 3.

Cost of Conflict in the Middle East

Sources, Annexures and Acknowledgements

SOURCES

Chapter 1: Economic Costs

Backgrounder
"Gross Domestic Product 2007." World Development Indicators Database, World Bank, 1 July 2008. http://siteresources.worldbank.org/DATASTATISTICS/Resources/GDP.pdf

"GDP at Current Prices – US Dollars." United Nations National Accounts Main Aggregates Database, United Nations Statistics Division, August 2007. http://unstats.un.org/unsd/snaama/selectionbasicFast.asp

"Statistical Appendix: Real GDP Growth." Regional Economic Outlook: Middle East and Central Asia, Pg. 34, International Monetary Fund (IMF), May 2007. http://www.imf.org/external/pubs/ft/reo/2007/MCD/ENG/mreo0507.pdf

"World Population Prospects: 2006 Revision." Population Division, United Nations Department of Economic and Social Affairs, 2006. http://esa.un.org/unpp/index.asp?panel=2

1. Opportunity Cost since Madrid
"GDP at Current Prices – US Dollars." United Nations National Accounts Main Aggregates Database, United Nations Statistics Division, August 2007. http://unstats.un.org/unsd/snaama/selectionbasicFast.asp

4. War, Civil War and Growth
United Nations National Accounts Main Aggregates Database, United Nations Statistics Division, August 2007. http://unstats.un.org/unsd/snaama/selectionbasicFast.asp

5. Cost of Iraq War
Stiglitz, Joseph and Linda Bilmes. "The Three Trillion Dollar War: The True Cost of the Iraq Conflict." New York: WW Norton & Co Inc, March 2008.

7. Travails of Host Countries
"UNHCR 2006 Statistical Yearbook: Trends in Displacement, Protection and Solutions." Switzerland: United Nations High Commission of Refugees (UNHCR), December 2007. http://www.unhcr.org/statistics/STATISTICS/478cda572.html

"Field Listings: Refugees and Internally Displaced Persons." CIA Fact-book, US Central Intelligence Agency, 2007. https://www.cia.gov/library/publications/the-world-factbook/fields/2194.html

Riera Jose and Andrew Harper. "Iraq the Search for Solutions." Iraq's Displacement Crisis: The Search for Solutions. Forced Migration Review (Special Issue), Refugee Studies Centre, Department of International Development, Oxford June 2007. http://www.fmreview.org/FMRpdfs/Iraq/full.pdf

8. Iraq, Iran and Oil
"World Crude Oil Production: 1970-2007 (thousand barrels per day)." International Petroleum Monthly, Energy Information Administration (EIA), 6 August 2008. http://www.eia.doe.gov/emeu/ipsr/t41b.xls

9. Israel Hezbollah Conflict in 2006
Kalman, Matthew. "Paying War's Toll: Northern Israel's tourism fades, but ceasefire raises hope." San Francisco Chronicle, 19 August 2006. http://www.sfchroniclemarketplace.com/cgi-bin/article.cgi?f=/c/a/2006/08/19/BUGD0KKBCR1.DTL

Elliman, Wendy. "From Despair to Opportunity: Rebuilding Northern Israel." Shalom, December 2006/January 2007.

Israel's Small Businesses Bear Brunt of War's Losses: But hostilities not expected to hurt nation's economy." Boston Globe, 27 July 2006. http://www.boston.com/news/world/middleeast/articles/2006/07/27/israels_small_businesses_bear_brunt_of_wars_losses/

Rosenblum, Irit. "War in Lebanon Cost Israel's Tourist Industry 500,000 Visitors." Haaretz, 20 December 2006. http://www.haaretz.co.il/hasen/pages/ShArtStEng.jhtml?itemNo=803516&contrassID=1&subContrassID=1&title='War%20in%20Lebanon%20cost%20Israel's%20tourist%20industry%20500,000%20visitors%20'&dyn_server=172.20.5.5

Borger, Julian. "Lebanon War Cost Israel $1.6 billion." The Guardian, 15 August 2006. http://www.guardian.co.uk/world/2006/aug/15/israelandthepalestinians.lebanon

Council for Development and Reconstruction, Government of Lebanon http://www.cdr.gov.lb/indexe.html

11. Asymmetrical Trade between Palestine and Israel
"Current Main Indicators: 2000-2005." Foreign Trade, Economic, Statistics. Palestinian Central Bureau for Statistics (PCBS), 2008. http://www.pcbs.gov.ps/DesktopDefault.aspx?tabID=3565&lang=en

Chapter 2: Military Costs

Backgrounder
"Fatalities." Statistics, B'Tselem, October 2008. http://www.btselem.org/english/statistics/Casualties.asp

"Documented Civilian Deaths by Violence." Iraq Body Court, 2008. http://www.iraqbodycount.org

"Iraq Index: Tracking variables of resconstruction and security in post-Saddam Iraq." Brookings Institution, October 2007. http://www.brookings.edu/fp/saban/iraq/index.pdf

White, Matthew. "Twentieth Century Atlas: Death Tolls." June 2005. http://users.erols.com/mwhite28/warstats.htm

"Iran-Iraq War (1980-1988)." Global Security. 2008. http://www.globalsecurity.org/military/world/war/iran-iraq.him

Also CNN, BBC, Reuters and CBS news reports

"Signatories and Parties on the Treaty to the Non-Proliferation of Nuclear Weapons." Federation of American Scientists (FAS), 3 December 1998. http://www.fas.org/nuke/control/npt/text/npt3.htm

"Status of Signature and Ratification." Preparatory Commission, Comprehensive Test Ban Treaty Organization (CTBTO), 2008. http://www.ctbto.org/the-treaty/status-of-signature-and-ratification/

2. Military Expenditure in the Middle East

"Military Expenditure by Country as Percentage of Gross Domestic Product, 1997-2005." Stockholm International Peace Research Institute (SIPRI) Yearbook 2007, Pg. 317-323, New York: Oxford University Press, 2007.

"Military Expenditure by Country, in Constant US Dollars for 1997-2006 and Current US Dollars for 2006." Stockholm International Peace Research Institute (SIPRI) Yearbook 2007, Pg. 310-316, New York: Oxford University Press, 2007.

3. Medicine and Military
"Military Expenditure by Country as Percentage of Gross Domestic Product, 1997-2005." Stockholm International Peace Research Institute (SIPRI) Yearbook 2007, Pg. 317-323, New York: Oxford University Press, 2007.

"Public Expenditure on Health (% of GDP)." Commitment to Health: resources, access and services. Human Development Report 2007-2008, UNHDR stats, United Nations Development Program (UNDP), 2008. http://hdrstats.undp.org/indicators/50.html

5. Militarization of the Society
"Capabilities:Active and Reserve." Military Balance 2006, Pgs. 182-213, International Institute for Strategic Studies (IISS). UK: Routledge, 2006.

6. Beyond Regulars and Reserves
"Capabilities:Active." Military Balance 2006, Pgs. 182-213, International Institute for Strategic Studies (IISS). UK: Routledge, 2006.

"Estimated Strength of Insurgency Nationwide." Iraq Index: Tracking variables of reconstruction and security in post-Saddam Iraq, Pg. 26, Saban Center for Middle East Policy, The Brookings Institution, 1 October 2007. http://www.brookings.edu/fp/saban/iraq/index.pdf

7. US Military Personnel
"Active Duty Military Personnel Strengths by Regional Area and by Country, (309A)." Washington Headquarters Services, Directorate for Information Operations and Reports, US Department of Defence, 30 September 1989. http:// siadapp.dmdc.osd.mil/personnel/Military/history/Hst0989.pdf

"United States: Deployment." Military Balance 2006, Pgs. 40-44, International Institute for Strategic Studies (IISS), UK: Routledge, 2006.

8. Nuclear Activity
"Iran: Nuclear Intentions and Capabilities." National Intelligence Estimate (NIE), November 2007. http://www.dni.gov/press_releases/20071203_release.pdf

"Iran: Weapons of Mass Destruction, Capabilities and Programs." Center for Non-Proliferation Studies, Monterey Institute of International Studies (MIIS), updated April 2006. http://cns.miis.edu/research/wmdme/iran.htm

Hassan, Hussein. "Iranian Nuclear Sites." CRS Report for Congress, Congressional Research Service (CRS), updated 9 August 2007. http://www.fas.org/sgp/crs/nuke/RS22531.pdf

"Israel: Weapons of Mass Destruction Capabilities and Programs." Center for Non-Proliferation Studies, Monterey Institute of International Studies(MIIS), updated April 2006. http://cns.miis.edu/research/wmdme/israel.htm

"Israel's Nuclear Programme." BBC WOrld News, 22 December 2003. http://news.bbc.co.uk/2/hi/middle_east/3340639.stm

"Israel: Uranium Processing and Enrichment." The Risk Report, Volume 2 Number 4, Wisconsin Project on Nuclear Arms Control, July-August 1996. http://www.wisconsinproject.org/countries/israel/uranium.html

"Egypt Profile: Nuclear, Chemical, Biological, Missile Overview." Nuclear Threat Initiative (NTI), October 2007. http://www.nti.org/e_research/profiles/Egypt/Nuclear/index.html

Gregory, Barbara. "Egypt's Nuclear Program: Assessing supplier-based and other developmental constraints." Center for Non-Proliferation Studies, Monterey Institute of International Studies (MIIS), Fall 1995. http://cns.miis.edu/npr/pdfs/gregor31.pdf

"Syria Profile: Nuclear, Chemical, Biological, Missile Overview." Nuclear Threat Initiative (NTI), September 2007. http://www.nti.org/e_research/profiles/Syria/index.html

Mahnaimi, Uzi and Sarah Baxter. "Israelis Seized Nuclear Material in Syrian Raid." The Sunday Times, 23 September 2007. http://www.timesonline.co.uk/tol/news/world/middle_east/article2512380.ece

"Syria: Nuclear Facilities Profile." Stockholm International Peace Research Institute (SIPRI), July 2004. http://www.sipri.org/contents/expcon/cnsc3syr.html

Sanger, David and Mark Mazetti. "Israel Struck Syrian Nuclear Project, Analysts Say." New York Times, 14 October 2007. http://www.nytimes.com/2007/10/14/washington/14weapons.html?fta=y

Pomper, Miles. "Israel, Neighbours Mull Nuclear Power Programs." Arms Control Association, September 2007. http://www.armscontrol.org/act/2007_09/Israel

Stern, Yoav. "Iranian Envoy Offers Egypt Cooperation on Nuclear Program." Haaretz, 30 December 2007. http://www.haaretz.com/hasen/spages/939831.html

Sokolski, Henry. "Atomic: Why are France and America Helping the Mideast Go Nuclear?" The Wall Street Journal, 17 January 2008. http://online.wsj.com/article/SB120052554733695743.html

"Turkey Postpones Nuclear Power Plant Tender." Turkish Weekly. February 2008.

Cirincione, Joseph and Yuri Leventer. "Recipe for War: The Middle East's nuclear surge." International Herald Tribune, 13 August 2007. http://www.iht.com/articles/2007/08/13/opinion/edcirin.php?page=2

"Algeria's Nuclear Secrecy." Insights: Energy and Environment, Energy Publisher, 31 July 2007. http://www.energypublisher.com/article.asp?id=10507

"Acquisition of Technology Relating to WMD and Advanced Conventional Munitions: Unclassified report to Congress from the director of Central Intelligence." The threat of a clandestine nuclear attack. Weapons of Mass Destruction: Intelligence threat assessment (Official documents), Federation of American Scientists (FAS), 30 January 2001 & 2006. http://www.fas.org/irp/threat/wmd.htm#clan

9. Missile Mania
"Worldwide Ballistic Missile Inventory: Fact Sheet." Arms Control Association, September 2007. http://www.armscontrol.org/factsheets/missiles

"Proposed ATACMS Sale to Bahrain Announced." Arms Control Today, Arms Control Association, October 2000. http://www.armscontrol.org/node/3017

Ochsenbein, Adrian. "Factsheet: Ballistic Missile Proliferation, year 2005 report." Defense Threat Information Group (DTIG), November 2005. http://www.dtig.org/docs/bm_deployment2005.pdf

Cowell, Alan and William Broad J. "Iran Reports Missile Test: Drawing rebuke." New York Times, 10 July 2008. http://www.nytimes.com/2008/07/10/world/asia/10iran.html?fta=y

"Iran Builds New Longer-range Missile." AFP, 26 November 2007. http://afp.google.com/article/ALeqM5gReGmLPkJw9ZkWLZT_Z9f_ynOvRA

"Iran: Weapons of Mass Destruction, Capabilities and Programs." Weapons of Mass Destruction in the Middle East, Center for Non-Proliferation Studies, Monterey Institute of International Studies (MIIS), updated April 2006. http://cns.miis.edu/research/wmdme/iran.htm

Clawson, Patrick. "Nuclear Proliferation in the Middle East: Who is next after Iran? Washington Institute for Near East Policy, April 2003. http://www.npec-<web.org/Essays/Presentation030401%20Clawson%20Nuclear%20Prolif%20TB.pdf

10. Nuclear Armageddon
"Cost of Conflict between India and Pakistan." International Centre for Peace Initiatives (ICPI), Strategic Foresight Group (SFG), 2004.

Chapter 3: Environmental Costs

Backgrounder
Fahimi-Roudeh, Farzaneh, Liz Creel and Roger-Mark De Souza. "Finding the Balance: Population and water scarcity in the Middle East and North Africa." Population Reference Bureau (PRB), July 2002. http://www.prb.org/Publications/PolicyBriefs/FindingtheBalancePopulationandWaterScarcityintheMiddleEastandNorthAfrica.aspx

"Total Renewable Water Resources, Per Capita (actual)." Aquastat Database Query, Food and Agricultural Organization of the United Nations (FAO), February 2008. http://www.fao.org/nr/water/aquastat/data/query/index.html

1. Spills, Flames and Wells of Wars
Poonian, Chris. "The Effects of the 1991 Gulf War on the Marine and Coastal Environment of the Arabian Gulf: Impact, recovery and the future." Kings College, London, 2003. http://www.c-3.org.uk/Multimedia/Reports/Gulf%20war_Poonian.pdf

Stead, Craig F. "Oil Fires, Petroleum and Gulf War Illness." Considered at the CDC conference on health impact of chemical exposures during the Gulf War, 1999. http://www.penfield-gill.com/presentations/CDCall-final.htm

Krupa, Melissa "Environmental and economic Repercussions of the Persian Gulf War on Kuwait." ICE Case Studies No. 9, American University, Washington DC, May 1997. http://www.american.edu/ted/ice/kuwait.htm

McClain MacLeod, Heather. "Oil Fires and Spills Leave Hazardous Legacy." The Unfinished War: A decade since desert storm. CNN in depth specials, 2000. http://edition.cnn.com/SPECIALS/2001/gulf.war/legacy/environment/index.html

Birdlife International. "Threats to the Environment Posed by War in Iraq." Science in Africa, http://www.scienceinafrica.co.za/2003/march/war.htm

"The Mesopotamian Marshlands: Demise of an Ecosystem." Early Warning and Assessment Technical Report. United Nations Environmental Program (UNEP), 2001. http://www.grid.unep.ch/activities/sustainable/tigris/mesopotamia.pdf

Shevtsov, Andriy. Environmental Implications of the 2006 Israel-Lebanon Conflict." ICE Case Studies No. 216, American University, Washington DC, May 2007. http://www.american.edu/ted/ice/lebanon-war.htm

"Press Release." Green Line Foundation, Lebanon. July 2006. http://www.greenline.org.lb/new/english/news20060727.html

"Lebanon: Post-Conflict Environmental Assessment." United Nations Environmental Program (UNEP), January 2007. http://www.unep.org/pdf/Lebanon_PCOB_Report.pdf

Israel Ministry of Environmental Protection. http://english.sviva.gov.il/Enviroment/bin/en.jsp?enPage=e_HomePage

"Desk Study on the Environment in Iraq." United Nations Environmental Program(UNEP). 2003. http://www.unep.org/pdf/iraq_ds.pdf

Dixon, Michelle and Spencer Fitz-Gibbon. "The Environmental Consequences of the War in Iraq." A Green Party Press Office Briefing. Ed. Grace Gedge. Green Party, UK, April 2003. http://www.greenparty.org.uk/files/reports/2003/The%20Environmental%20Consequences%20of%20the%20War%20on%20Iraq%202.doc

2. Depleted Uranium Shells
"Iraq Weapons of Mass Destruction Programs." U.S. Government White Paper. Federation of American Scientists (FAS), released 13 February 1998. http://www.fas.org/irp/threat/whitepap.htm

3. War and Water
"Communicable disease profile: Iraq." World Health Organization (WHO), updated 19 March 2003. http://www.who.int/infectious-disease-news/IDdocs/whocds200317/1profile.pdf

Dore, Lucia. "Per Capita Water Availability in the Middle East to Fall by 50 Percent." Business Times, Khaleej Times. 7 October 2007. http://www.middleeastelectricity.com/upl_images/news/Per-capita-water-availability-in%C2%AD-the-MiddleEast-to-fall-by-50percent.pdf

Normand, Roger. "Water Under Siege in Iraq." Centre for Economic and Social Rights (CESR), 2003. http://cesr.org/node/18

Nagy, Thomas J. "How the US Deliberately Destroyed Iraq's Water Center for Research on Globalization." Centre for Research on Globalization, 29 August 2001. http://www.globalresearch.ca/articles/NAG108A.html

Conetta, Carl. "Reconstructing Iraq: Costs and possible income sources." Project on Defence Alternatives. Briefing Memo No. 28. Commonwealth Institute, 25 April 2003. http://www.uslaboragainstwar.org/article.php?id=3460

"Rebuilding Iraq: US water and sanitation efforts need improved measures for assessing impact and sustained resources for maintaining facilities." Report to Congressional Committee. United States Government Accountability Office (GAO), September 2005. http://www.gao.gov/new.items/d05872.pdf

"Paying for Iraq's Reconstruction." Congressional Budget Office, The Congress of the United States, January 2004. http://www.cbo.gov/doc.cfm?index=4983

"Lebanon: Water supply is a Priority Issue for the South." IRIN news, 12 March 2007. http://www.irinnews.org/Report.aspx?ReportId=70642

"Higher Relief Commission: Daily Situation Report." Lebanonundersiege. Government of Lebanon, 16 October 2006. http://www.lebanonundersiege.gov.lb/images_Browse/00000642_situation%20report%2075.doc

"Lebanon: Post-Conflict Environmental Assessment." United Nations Environmental Program (UNEP). January 2007. http://www.unep.org/pdf/Lebanon_PCOB_Report.pdf

4. Warning: Water Wars Ahead
"Dependency Ratio (%)." Aquastat Database Query. Food and Agricultural Organization of the United Nations (FAO), 1988-2007.

Fisher, Franklin M. and Hossein Askari. "Optimal Water Management in the Middle East and Other Regions." Finance and Development. Volume 38, No. 3, International Monetary Fund (IMF), Sept. 2001. http://www.imf.org/external/pubs/ft/fandd/2001/09/fisher.htm

"Country Profiles." Country and Region, Aquastat. Food and Agricultural Organization of the United Nations (FAO), February 2007. http://www.fao.org/nr/water/aquastat/countries/index.stm

Isaac, Jad. "The Palestinian Water Crisis." Palestine Center, 14 August 1999. http://www.palestinecenter.org/cpap/pubs/19990818ib.html

"General Summary Near East Region." Aquastat. Food and Agricultural Organization of the United Nations (FAO), January 2008. http://www.fao.org/nr/water/aquastat/regions/neast/index3.stm

"Water & Environment." PASSIA Facts, PASSIA journal 2006-2007. Palestinian Academic Society for the Study of International Affairs (PASSIA), 2007. http://209.85.175.104/search?q=cache:2aVWusUdMSQJ:www.passia.org/palestine_facts/pdf/pdf2006/7-Water-Environment.doc+Water+and+Environment%2BPASSIA&hl=en&ct=clnk&cd=1&gl=in

Murakami, Masahiro. "Managing Water for Peace in the Middle East: Alternative Strategies." United Nations University Press, 1995. http://www.unu.edu/unupress/unupbooks/80858e/80858e00.htm

5. Attacks on Desalination Plants in Future Conflicts
Spang, Edward. "The Potential for Wind-Powered Desalination in Water-Scarce Countries." Fletcher School, Tufts University, 7 February 2006. http://fletcher.tufts.edu/research/2006/Spang.pdf

"General Summary Near East Region." Aquastat. Food and Agricultural Organization of the United Nations (FAO), January 2008. http://www.fao.org/nr/water/aquastat/regions/neast/index3.stm

6. Carbon Emissions in a Future War
"Carbon Emissions from energy use and cement manufacturing, 1850 to 2000." World Resources Institute, 2003. http://www.nationmaster.com/graph/env_co2_emi-environment-co2-emissions

7. Loss of Bio-diversity
"Birdlife Leads Iraq Project." Birdlife International, 19 April 2006. http://www.birdlife.org/news/news/2006/04/iraq.html

8. Agriculture
De Chatel, Francesca. "Water Sheikhs & Dam Builders: Stories of People and Water in the Middle East." New Jersey: Transaction Publishers, 2007.

"Damage to Agriculture, Fisheries and Forestry Estimated at Around $280 Million." FAO Newsroom. Food and Agriculture Organization of the United Nations (FAO), 27 November 2006. http://www.fao.org/Newsroom/en/news/2006/1000445/index.html

"Lebanon: Controlling Food Prices." Oxford Business Group, 3 July 2008. http://www.zawya.com/Story.cfm/sidZAWYA20080703132622/SecCountries/pagLebanon/chnLebanon%20Analysis/objA68CBE92-8400-11D5-867D00D-0B74A0D7C/

9. Impact of Climate Change
Freimuth, Ladeene, Gidon Bromberg, Munqeth Mehyar and Nader Al Khateeb. "Climate Change: A new threat to Middle East Security.", Friends of the Earth Middle East, December 2007. http://www.foeme.org/index_images/dinamicas/publications/publ78_1.pdf

Climate Change and Water Resources in the Middle East: Vulnerability, Socio-Economic Impacts, and Adaptation El-Fadel, M. and E. Bou Zeid, Fondazione Eni Enrico Mattei, June 2001. http://www.feem.it/NR/rdonlyres/7EAE52F3-44AD-4F9A-AA9A-9899AED8F203/432/4601.pdf

Chapter 4: Social and Political Costs

Backgrounder
"International Religious Freedom Report 2007." Bureau of Democracy, Human Rights, and Labor, U.S. State Department. 14 September 2007. http://www.state.gov/g/drl/rls/irf/2007/

2. Religion in Politics
"Field Listing – Legislative Branch: Egypt: 2005 Elections." The World Factbook. United States Central Intelligence Agency (CIA), August 2008. https://www.cia.gov/library/publications/the-world-factbook/fields/2101.html

"Encyclopedia: Elections in Egypt: 2005 elections." NationMaster. http://www.nationmaster.com/encyclopedia/Elections-in-Egypt

"National Results: Elections for the 17th Knesset." Knesset Website. 2006. http://www.knesset.gov.il/elections17/eng/Results/main_results_eng.asp

"The Final Results of the Electoral Lists.", Central Elections Commission - Palestine, 29 January 2001. http://www.elections.ps/template.aspx?id=291

"Final Report on the Parliamentary Elections." European Union Election Observation Mission to Lebanon 2005. Pg. 40, European Union, 2005. http://ec.europa.eu/external_relations/human_rights/eu_election_ass_observ/lebanon/final_report.pdf

Ridolfo, Kathleen. "Iraq: Election Commission Releases Final Vote Results." Global Security, 20 January 2006. http://www.globalsecurity.org/wmd/library/news/iraq/2006/01/iraq-060120-rferl02.htm

Al-Qatari, Hussain. "Elections 2008 Guide." Kuwait Times, 17 May 2008.

http://www.kuwaittimes.net/read_news.php?newsid=OTE4MzA3MDE4

"Field Listing – Legislative Branch: Kuwait: 2008 Elections." The World Factbook. United States Central Intelligence Agency (CIA). August 2008. https://www.cia.gov/library/publications/the-world-factbook/fields/2101.html

Worth, Robert F. "Islamists win 24 of 50 Seats in Parliament of Kuwait." New York Times, 19 May 2008. http://www.nytimes.com/2008/05/19/world/middleeast/19kuwait.html?ref=middleeast

"Field Listing – Legislative Branch: Jordan: 2007 Elections." The World Factbook. United States Central Intelligence Agency (CIA), August 2008. https://www.cia.gov/library/publications/the-world-factbook/fields/2101.html

3. Freedom of Press
"Annual Worldwide Press Freedom Index: 2003-2007." Reporters without Borders. http://www.rsf.org/article.php3?id_article=24025

4. Curbs on Civil Liberties
"Freedom in the World: 2008 Survey." Freedom House, 2 July 2008. http://www.freedomhouse.org/template.cfm?page=395

Association for Civil Rights in Israel. www.acri.org.il

"Jerusalem: the Eastside Story", documentary film by Mohammed Alatar. http://www.eastsidestory.ps/diduknow.shtml

5. Children's Condition
"Core Indicators in Depth: Education, Water, Child Nutrition, Child Survival & Health." United Nations Children Fund (UNICEF), December 2007. http://www.unicef.org/statistics/index_24296.html

"The State of the World's Children." United Nations Children Fund (UNICEF), December 2007. http://www.unicef.org/sowc08/docs/sowc08.pdf

"Little Respite for Iraq's Children in 2008." United Nations Children Fund (UNICEF), 21 December 2007. http://www.uniraq.org/documents/State%20of%20Iraqs%20Children%20PR_181207_EN.pdf

"UN Reports Children Used as Combatants in Iraq." CNN International, 19 January 2006. http://edition.cnn.com/2006/WORLD/meast/01/18/iraq.rights/index.html

"Women, Children and Youth in the Iraq Crisis: A Fact Sheet." Women's Commission. Refugee Human Rights Commission (RHRC), January 2008. http://www.rhrc.org/pdf/Iraqi_women_girls_factsheet%20FINAL%20JAn08.pdf

"Report of the Secretary General to the General Assembly of the Security Council." Sixty Second session Agenda Item 66 (a). Children in Armed Conflict, 21 December 2007. http://daccessdds.un.org/doc/UNDOC/GEN/N07/656/04/PDF/N0765604.pdf?OpenElement

Jonathan, Ashley. "Trapped! The Disappearing Hopes of the Iraqi Refugee Children." World Vision, April 2007. http://meero.worldvision.org/docs/57.pdf

"Visit of the Special Representatives to Lebanon." Information based on the 2006 Report of the Secretary General to the Security Council. Children and Armed Conflict, 26 October 2006. http://www.un.org/children/conflict/english/lebanon-and-israel.html

Alami, Mona. "Lebanon: Peace Brings no Joy to Children." Inter Press Service (IPS), 4 March 2008. http://ipsnews.net/news.asp?idnews=41448

"Lebanon: Displaced Again." Internal Displacement Monitoring Centre (IDMC), 23 July 2008. http://www.internal-displacement.org/8025708F004CE90B/(httpCountries)/99D28A56726B48B9802570A7004CCFD8?OpenDocument&expand=6.1&link=27.6.1&count=10000#27.6.1

6. Conscription
Hadass, Yael S. "On the Causes of Military Conscription." Social Science Research Network (SSRN), 21 June 2004. http://papers.ssrn.com/sol3/papers.cfm?abstract_id=564062

Horeman, Bart and Mark Stolwijk. "The Refusal to Bear Arms: A world survey on conscription and conscientious objection to military service." War Resisters International, 1998. http://www.wri-irg.org/co/rtba/index.html

7. Sectarian Strife
"Multiple Fatality Bombings by Sectarian Groups - Iraq." Iraq Index: Tracking variables of reconstruction and security in post-Saddam Iraq, Pg. 12, Saban Center for Middle East Policy, The Brookings Institution, 1 October 2007. http://www.brookings.edu/fp/saban/iraq/index.pdf

"International Religious Freedom Report 2007." Bureau of Democracy, Human Rights, and Labor, U.S. State Department, 14 September 2007. http://www.state.gov/g/drl/rls/irf/2007/

"Country Profiles: Middle East: Population." BBC World News, last updated 27 August 2008. http://news.bbc.co.uk/1/hi/world/middle_east/country_profiles/790877.stm

"Field Listing: Ethnic Groups." World Factbook. United States Central Intelligence Agency (CIA), 2007. https://www.cia.gov/library/publications/the-world-factbook/fields/2075.html

8. Crash of Civilization
Jury, Louise. "At Least 8,000 Treasures Looted from Iraq Museum Still Untraced." The Independent, 24 May 2005. http://www.globalpolicy.org/security/issues/iraq/attack/consequences/2005/0524treasures.htm

Gugliotta, Guy. "Looted Iraqi Relics Slow to Surface: Some famous pieces unlikely to reappear." Washington Post, 8 November 2005. http://www.globalpolicy.org/security/issues/iraq/attack/consequences/2005/1108relics.htm

Woolf, Marie. "Desecration of the Cradle of Civilisation." The Independent, 15 April 2007. http://www.independent.co.uk/news/uk/this-britain/desecration-of-the-cradle-of-civilisation-444775.html

"Cultural Heritage Reference Group for Iraq: Final Report." United Nations Education and Cultural Organization (UNESCO), 20 April 2003. http://209.85.175.104/search?q=cache:WJXueDtm6MwJ:www.aph.gov.au/SENATE/COMMITTEE/ecita_ctte/estimates/add_0506/eh/hd_q32att_a.rtf+Verbal+report+by+Dr+Donny+George,+Director+of+Research,+Iraqi+Museum,+UNESCO,+2003&hl=en&ct=clnk&cd=3&gl=in

"World Survey of Islamic Manuscripts." Vol. 2 G., ed. Roper, 1993.

9. Global Image
"Rising Environmental Concerns in 47 Nation Survey." The Pew Global Attitudes Survey. Pgs 47 & 55. Pew Global Attitudes Project, Pew Research Center, 27 June 2007. http://pewglobal.org/reports/pdf/256.pdf

"The Rift Between Muslims and the West: Causes and Consequences." The Great Divide: How Westerners and Muslims View Each Other, Europe's Muslims more moderate. Pew Global Attitudes Project, Pew Research Center, 22 June 2006. http://pewglobal.org/reports/display.php?PageID=830

10. Iraq's Crisis of Education
"Situation Analysis of Education in Iraq 2003." United Nations Education, Cultural and Scientific Organization (UNESCO), Paris, April 2003. http://unesdoc.unesco.org/images/0013/001308/130838e.pdf

"Iraqi Education System Caught in Crossfire of Continued Conflict." Iraq in Transition- Background Report. PBS, 12 February 2007. http://www.pbs.org/newshour/indepth_coverage/middle_east/iraq/jan-june07/infrastructure_02-12.html

O'Malley, Brendan. "Education Under Attack." UNESCO, Paris, April 2007. http://unesdoc.unesco.org/images/0015/001505/150548e.pdf

Sarhan, Afif. "Iraq's Collapsing Education." Islam Online, 26 March 2008. http://www.islamonline.net/servlet/Satellite?c=Article_C&pagename=Zone-English-News/NWELayout&cid=1203758415260

Also see "Iraq's Education System on the Verge of Collapse." For case studies and personal accounts of academics killed. http://www.globalresearch.ca/index.php?context=viewArticle&code=ADR20070418&articleId=5429

11. Education Costs of Lebanon's 2006 War
"Lebanon Takes a Vital Step in Post-Conflict Recovery as Students Return to School." UNICEF and Ministry of Education, 17 October 2006. http://www.unicef.org/media/media_36180.html

"Lebanon's Education System Receives $2.7 Million Grant." Lebanon Under Seige, 9 July 2007. http://www.lebanonundersiege.gov.lb/english/F/eNews/NewsArticle.asp?CNewsID=999

"Developments in Lebanon and Israel: Visit of the special representative to Lebanon." Children in Armed Conflict, 26 October 2006. http://www.un.org/children/conflict/english/lebanon-and-israel.html

Chapter 5: Costs for the Palestinian People

1. Human Costs
"Palestinian Fatalities Since the Beginning of the Al Aqsa Intifada: A monthly list of Palestinians killed since 29 September 2000." Al Aqsa Intifada. The Palestinian Human Rights Monitoring Group, Sept. 2000 –Aug. 2008. http://www.phrmg.org/aqsa/fatalities_list.htm

"Who is Responsible for the Civilian Casualties during the Intifada? Israel 1991 to Present: Intifada Caualties. Palestine Facts, 2008. http://www.palestinefacts.org/pf_1991to_now_alaqsa_casualties.php

"Five Years of Al-Aqsa Intifada." Arabic Media Internet Network (AMIN), 28 September 2005. http://www.amin.org/look/amin/en.tpl?IdLanguage=1&IdPublication=7&NrArticle=34051&NrIssue=1&NrSection=3

"60 Years: Palestinian Nakba 1948." PASSIA Diary 2008, Pgs. 331-332, Palestinian Academic Society for the Study of International Affairs (PASSIA), 2008.

"Economic and Social Repercussions of the Israeli Occupation on the Living conditions of the Palestinian People…" General Assembly 63rd Session. United Nations Social and Economic Council, 6 May 2008. http://domino.un.org/unispal.nsf/9a798adbf322aff38525617b006d88d7/c7ed9f55068f00ee85257464004a5679!OpenDocument

Hasselknippe, Gro and Marianne Tveit. "Against the Odds." FAFO Report 2007:41, Oslo, 2007. http://www.fafo.no/pub/rapp/20041/index.html
(also recommend all FAFO reports containing analysis of living conditions and labour markets in the Palestine territories, Syria, Jordan and Iraq. www.fafo.no/english/)

2. Poverty
"Prolonged Crisis in the Occupied Palestinian Territories: Recent Socio-Economic Impacts of the New Phase on Refugees and Non-Refugees. Gaza." United Nations Relief and Works Agency (UNRWA), November 2006. http://www.un.org/unrwa/news/SocioEconomicImpacts_Nov06.pdf

"The Gaza Strip: A Humanitarian Implosion." OXFAM, March 2008. http://www.oxfam.org.uk/resources/downloads/oxfam_gaza_lowres.pdf

3. Israeli Settlements
"The Situation of Workers of the Occupied Arab Territories." Report of the Director General at the International Labor Session, 95th Session 2006. Pg. 16, International Labor Office (ILO) Geneva, 2006. http://www.reliefweb.int/rw/RWFiles2006.nsf/FilesByRWDocUnidFilename/HMYT-6Q6MS5-ilo-opt-26may.pdf/$File/ilo-opt-26may.pdf

"60 Years: Palestinian Nakba 1948." PASSIA Diary 2008, Pg. 343, Palestinian Academic Society for the Study of International Affairs (PASSIA), 2008.

Foundation for the Middle East. http://www.fmep.org/settlement_info/settlement-info-and-tables/stats-data/comprehensive-settlement-population-1972-2006

"Palestinians: Number of West Bank settlers jumped nearly 4% in 2007" in Haaretz, August 14, 2008

4. Stagnant Health Services
"Number of Hospitals, Beds and Beds per 1,000 Populations in the Palestinian Territory in the Mid Year by Region 1996-2005." Palestinian Central Bureau of Statistics (PCBS). http://www.pcbs.gov.ps/Portals/_pcbs/health/tab3.htm

"Specific Health Indicators in the Palestinian Territory 1996-2005." Palestinian Bureau of Statistics (PCBS). http://www.pcbs.gov.ps/Portals/_pcbs/health/tab1.htm

"60 Years: Palestinian Nakba 1948." PASSIA Diary 2008, Pg. 362, Palestinian Academic Society for the Study of International Affairs (PASSIA), 2008.

6. Death of Childhood
"Israeli Violations of the Right to Life: Palestinian child fatalities in the Occupied Palestinian Territory during the first half of the year 2007." Defence for Children International (DCI), Palestine Section. 2007. http://www.dci-pal.org/english/doc/reports/2007/nov10.pdf

7. Education Lost
Nicolai, Susan. "Education and Chronic Crisis in Palestine." FMR Education Supplement. Forced Migration Review (FMR). 2008. http://www.fmreview.org/FMRpdfs/EducationSupplement/16.pdf

"The Gaza Strip: A Humanitarian Implosion." OXFAM, March 2008. http://www.oxfam.org.uk/resources/downloads/oxfam_gaza_lowres.pdf

8. Troubled Farmlands
"Rehabilitation of Destroyed Agricultural Lands in Eastern Gaza." The Agricultural Development Association (PARC) –Gaza. September 2007. http://www.apnature.org/articles/41.doc

"60 Years: Palestinian Nakba 1948." PASSIA Diary 2008, Pg. 349, 354 and 355, Palestinian Academic Society for the Study of International Affairs (PASSIA), 2008.

9. Unemployment
"Indicators of the Labour Force in the Palestinian Territory." On the Occasion of May 1 – International Worker's Day. Palestinian Central Bureau of Statistics (PCBS), 2006. http://www.pcbs.gov.ps/Portals/_pcbs/PressRelease/worker_e.pdf

Note: Employment data for workers in Israel includes employment in Israel settlements and industrial estates. West Bank data includes East Jerusalem, World Bank Group.

"60 Years: Palestinian Nakba 1948." PASSIA Diary 2008, Pg. 352-353, Palestinian Academic Society for the Study of International Affairs (PASSIA), 2008.

10. Jobless in Gaza
"The Gaza Strip: A Humanitarian Implosion." OXFAM, March 2008. http://www.oxfam.org.uk/resources/downloads/oxfam_gaza_lowres.pdf

"The Closure of the Gaza Strip: The economic and humanitarian consequences." OCHA Special Focus, occupied Palestinian territory. United Nations Office for the Coordination of Humanitarian Affairs (OCHA), December 2007. http://www.caremiddleeast.org/Linked%20pdf%20documents/Gaza_Special_Focus_December_2007.pdf

"Continued Commercial Closure of Gaza Will Cause Complete Humanitarian Dependency, Groups Warn." Oxfam Press Release. Arabic Media internet Network (AMIN), 22 July, 2007. http://www.amin.org/look/amin/en.tpl?IdLanguage=1&IdPublication=7&NrArticle=41477&NrIssue=1&NrSection=3

11. Withheld Taxes
"60 Years: Palestinian Nakba 1948." PASSIA Diary 2008, Pg. 356, Palestinian Academic Society for the Study of International Affairs (PASSIA), 2008.

12. Barriers and Closures
"West Bank Closure Count and Analysis', United Nations Office for the Coordination of Humanitarian Affairs (OCHA), January 2006. http://www.humanitarianinfo.org/opt/docs/UN/OCHA/OCHAoPt_ClosureAnalysis0106_En.pdf

Mahmoud Labadi: Former Director of Aid Coordination Department and UN Specialized Agencies in Palestine.

"Palestinians Who Died Following an Infringement of the Right to Medical Treatment." B'Tselem, 2007. http://www.btselem.org/English/Statistics/Casualties_Data.asp?Category=21

13. West Bank Wall
"60 Years: Palestinian Nakba 1948." PASSIA Diary 2008, Pg. 344, Palestinian Academic Society for the Study of International Affairs (PASSIA), 2008.

14. Demolition of Houses
"Demolition for Alleged Military Purposes: Statistics on houses demolished for alleged military purposes." B'Tselem, 2004-2007. http://www.btselem.org/english/Razing/Statistics.asp

15. Identity Cards
"60 Years: Palestinian Nakba 1948." PASSIA Diary 2008, Pg. 383, Palestinian Academic Society for the Study of International Affairs (PASSIA), 2008.

16. Refugees
"60 Years: Palestinian Nakba 1948." PASSIA Diary 2008, Pg. 337, Palestinian Academic Society for the Study of International Affairs (PASSIA), 2008.

"The Wandering Palestinians." The Economist, 8 May 2008. http://www.economist.com/world/mideast-africa/displaystory.cfm?story_id=11332217

17. Black-Out in Gaza
"Gaza humanitarian Situation Report: Power shortages in the Gaza Strip." United Nations Office for Coordination and Humanitarian Affairs (OCHA), 8 January 2008. http://domino.un.org/UNISPAL.NSF/22f431edb91c6f54852567 8a0051be1d/ddf01691bbb85ec3852573cb004fe90e!OpenDocument

"The Gaza Strip: A Humanitarian Implosion." OXFAM, March 2008. http://www.oxfam.org.uk/resources/downloads/oxfam_gaza_lowres.pdf

"60 Years: Palestinian Nakba 1948." PASSIA Diary 2008, Pg. 363-364, Palestinian Academic Society for the Study of International Affairs (PASSIA), 2008.

18. Water Woes
"60 Years: Palestinian Nakba 1948." PASSIA Diary 2008, Pg. 346, Palestinian Academic Society for the Study of International Affairs (PASSIA), 2008.

Isaac, Jad. "The Palestinian Water Crisis." Palestine Center, 14 August 1999. http://www.palestinecenter.org/cpap/pubs/19990818ib.html

Chapter 6: Costs to Israel

Backgrounder
Concepts from: Sneh, Ephraim. "Navigating Perilous Waters." Routlege Curzon, 2005.

1. Human Costs
"Casualties in Arab-Israeli Wars." Jewish Virtual Library: Division of the American-Israeli Cooperative Enterprise, 2008. http://www.jewishvirtuallibrary.org/jsource/History/casualties.html

"Israeli Casualties in Battle." Jewish Virtual Library: Division of the American-Israeli Cooperative Enterprise, 2008. http://www.jewishvirtuallibrary.org/jsource/History/casualty_table.html

"Fatalities" Statistics. B'Tselem, 2008. http://www.btselem.org/english/Statistics/Casualties.asp

2. Cafes, Schools and Bombs
"Israeli Minors killed by Palestinians in Israel." Fatality Statistics. B'Tselem, 2000-2008. http://www.btselem.org/English/Statistics/Casualties_month_table.asp?Category=16&region=ISRAEL

"Israeli Minors Killed by Palestinians in the Occupied Territories." Fatality Statistics. B'Tselem, 2000-2008. http://www.btselem.org/English/Statistics/Casualties_month_table.asp?Category=15&region=TER

Roffe-Ofir, Sharon. "New Program Battles Northern Children's War Trauma." Ynet news.com, 12 June 2008. http://www.ynetnews.com/articles/0,7340,L-3567192,00.html

"The Impact of Conflict on Children in Occupied Palestinian Territory and Israel." Watchlist on Children and Armed Conflict. Watchlist, 13 September 2002. http://www.watchlist.org/reports/files/israel.report.php

"Israel Arrests Palestinians Planning to Bomb School." VOA News & Ha'aretz, December 2003. http://www.highbeam.com/doc/1G1-110828756.html

Reeves, Phil. "Israel Strikes Back After School Bus Bomb Outrage." The Independent, 21 December 2000. http://www.independent.co.uk/news/world/middle-east/israel-strikes-back-after-school-bus-bomb-outrage-623069.html

3. Missile Attacks
Pipes, Daniel. "14 Terrorist Attacks a Day Against Israel." danielpipes.org, updated 8 January 2008. http://www.danielpipes.org/blog/2005/09/fourteen-terrorist-attacks-a-day-against.html

Intelligence and Terrorism Information Centre at the Intelligence Heritage & Commemoration Centre. http://www.terrorism-info.org.il/

4. Fear Psychosis
"The National Resilience Project." The Center for the Study of National Security, University of Haifa, 2000-2004. http://nssc.haifa.ac.il/files/Resilience%20Project.htmv

5. Economic Damage
"Economic Indicators." International Monetary Fund (IMF), 2008. http://www.imf.org

6. Battleground Experience for the Big Boss
History: List of former Prime Ministers. Prime Ministers Office, 2008. http://www.pmo.gov.il/PMOEng/History/FormerPrimeMinister/

"Yitzak Rabin: The Nobel Peace Prize 1994." Nobel Prize.org, 2008. http://nobelprize.org/nobel_prizes/peace/laureates/1994/rabin-

"Shimon Peres: The Nobel Peace Prize 1994." Nobel Prize.org, 2008. http://nobelprize.org/nobel_prizes/peace/laureates/1994/peres-bio.html

Knesset, Government of Israel, 2008. http://www.knesset.gov.il

Ministry of Foreign Affairs, Government of Israel, 2008. http://www.mfa.gov.il

7. Image Loss
"BBC World Service Poll: Israel and Iran share most negative ratings in global poll." BBC World News, 6 March 2007. http://news.bbc.co.uk/1/shared/bsp/hi/pdfs/06_03_07_perceptions.pdf

"Israel at 60 in the UK Media - an analysis." Just Journalism, April and May 2008. http://www.justjournalism.com/plugins/p1999_media_special_articles/pdf/1504_Israel60Booklet_05.pdf

8. Loss of Tourism
"Tourism in Israel 2006." Statistilite No.71. Israel Central Bureau of Statistics, 2008. http://www1.cbs.gov.il/reader/tayar_miuhad/miuhad_nosim_new_eng.html

Swirski, Shlomo. "Tourist Entries: Israel and neighbouring countries in millions." The Cost of Occupation: the burden of the Israeli-Palestinian conflict, 2008 Report. Advai Center, June 2008. http://www.adva.org/UserFiles/File/costofoccupation2008fullenglish(1).pdf

10. Price of Occupation
Hever, Shir. "Bulletin 2: The Settlements – Economic Costs to Israel." The Alternative Information Center, 17 August 2005. http://www.alternativenews.org/aic-publications/the-economy-of-the-occupation/bulletin-2-the-settlements---economic-cost-to-israel-20050817_2.html

Hever, Shir. "The Economy of the Occupation Part 2: The Settlements – Economic Costs to Israel." The Alternative Information Center, July 2005. http://www.alternativenews.org/images/stories/downloads/socioeconomic_bulletin_02.pdf

11. Slump in House Prices
"House price uncertainty continues in Israel." Global Property Guide. August 2008. http://www.globalpropertyguide.com/Middle-East/Israel/Price-History

12. Browning of Green Zones
Orenstein, Daniel. "Environment in Israel." Watson Institute for International Studies, Brown University. 2007. http://www.hillel.org/NR/rdonlyres/C0B-C2A85-5AEF-4590-9990-0AF6C842FF78/0/israel_global_environmentalism.pdf

Chapter 7: Benefits of Warm Peace

1. Israel's Peace Dividend
Hellman, Ziv Preparing for the Morning After, in Jerusalem Report, September 1, 2008

2. Arab Peace Dividend
Hellman, Ziv Preparing for the Morning After, in Jerusalem Report, September 1, 2008

"United Nations/World Bank Joint Iraq Needs Assessment." United Nations and World Bank, October 2003. http://siteresources.worldbank.org/IRFFI/Resources/Joint+Needs+Assessment.pdf

3. Promise of the Sinai Underground World
Rahman, Hatem Abdel. "Evaluation of Groundwater Resources in Lower Cretaceous Aquifer System in Sinai." Water Resources Management Journal, June 2001, Vol 15 (3), 2001. http://www.springerlink.com/content/p7793584 17213702/?p=9e555aa4738f47cb908a1eb013115080&pi=2

4. Railways
"Israeli Part of Hedjaz Railway to be Rebuilt." International Railway Journal, February 2005. http://findarticles.com/p/articles/mi_m0BQQ/is_2_45/ai_n10301107

"Government Authorizes Resurrection of Jezreel Valley Railway." Itim and Haaretz, 7 Sept 2006. http://www.haaretz.com/hasen/pages/ShArt.jhtml?itemNo=736302

Peres, Shimon. "Valley of Peace." IsraCast. 10 August 2007. http://www.isracast.com/article.aspx?ID=756&t=Valley-of-Peace---By-Shimon-Peres

Nissim, Gal. "Israel Railways Plans Lines to Gaza and Jenin" Israel Business News, Globes. 31 March 2005. http://www.skyscrapercity.com/archive/index.php?t-196972.html

5. Gas Deal between Israel, Palestine and British Gas
Krieger, Matthew. "British Gas, Israel to Freeze Hamas Out of $4 Billion Gas Deal." Jerusalem Post. 5 July 2007. http://www.jpost.com/servlet/Satellite?cid=1183459207651&pagename=JPost%2FJPArticle%2FShowFull

"UK Firm Seeking Gaza Gas Deal." Global Research. 25 May 2007. http://www.globalresearch.ca/index.php?context=va&aid=5759

Houk, Marian. "Outlines of a Grand Deal-Israel, Egypt, Gaza-taking shape." American Chronicle. 20 March 2008. http://www.americanchronicle.com/articles/55920

Krieger, Matthew. "Still Waters" Jerusalem Post. 16 August 2007. http://www.jpost.com/servlet/Satellite?cid=1186557463046&pagename=JPost%2FJPArticle%2FPrinter

6. Aqaba Peace Zone
"Jordan Offers Israel Use of Aqaba Airport." Israel Business Today. 30 June 1997. http://findarticles.com/p/articles/mi_hb4803/is_199706/ai_n17439476

Jordan, Amir. "Israel and Jordan Plan Joint Aqaba Airport." Jerusalem Post. 22 June 2006. http://www.standwithus.com/news_post.asp?NPI=863

"Gulf of Aqaba Transportation." Israel Ministry of Foreign Affairs. 30 September 1997. http://www.mfa.gov.il/MFA/Peace%20Process/Regional%20Projects/Gulf%20of%20Aqaba-%20Transportation

7. Peace Canal
Shafy, Samiha. "Israel-Jordan Project Aims to save Dead Sea." Spiegel Online. 5 September 2007. http://www.spiegel.de/international/world/0,1518,503953,00.html

Urquhart, Conal. "Peace Canal Deal for Thirsty Middle East." Guardian. 9 May 2005. http://www.guardian.co.uk/world/2005/may/09/israel1

"French, British Firms Win Contracts to Study Dead Sea Canal Project." Monsters and Critics.com. 23 March 2008. http://www.monstersandcritics.com/news/business/news/printer_1396545.php

10. Palestinian Stock Exchange
Bahour, Sam. "PSE Reflects Palestine's Extraordinary Circumstances." Bitter Lemons -International. Edition 2, Volume 6, 10 January 2008. http://www.bitterlemons-international.org/previous.php?opt=1&id=210#863

Mackay, Mairi. "Palestinians battle for stock market success." CNN. 7 May 2008. http://edition.cnn.com/2008/BUSINESS/05/02/securitiesexchange.mme/index.html

"This week on marketplace Middle East" CNN. 30 April 2008. http://edition.cnn.com/2008/BUSINESS/09/04/show.september5/index.html

"Palestine Securities Exchange Performance-2007: Struggling against the current." Global Investment House, Global Research. February 2008. http://www.globalinv.net/research/PSE-Performance-2007.pdf

11. FMCG sector in Palestine
Intajuna Project, Solutions for Development Consulting Co., Palestine, 2007. http://www.solutionsdev.ps/media.php

Shikoh, Rafi-uddin. "Potential of the Palestinian Private Sector in Crisis." Dinar Standard. 20 September 2007. http://dinarstandard.com/current/PaletineEcon_02_092007.htm

13. Investment Potential in the Palestinian Territories
"Business and Investment Opportunities: Palestine Authority." Medibtikar. 13 March 2007. http://www.medibtikar.eu/-Business-and-investment-.html?PHPSESSID=1529c85544fb2718fb2862ec04b6c64e

"Deals Signed as Palestinians Seek foreign Investment." Star Tribune. 21 May 2008. http://www.startribune.com/world/19161329.html?location_refer=Homepage

Bannoura, Ghassan. "Saudi Company to Invest $250 million in a Project in Palestine." The International Middle East Media Center. 22 May 2008. http://www.imemc.org/article/54993

"Qatari Diar Signs Deal for Palestinian Housing Projects." The Peninsula. 22 May 2008. http://www.thepeninsulaqatar.com/Display_news.asp?section=business_news&month=may2008&file=business_news2008052263234.xml

"Bethlehem Investment Conference Raises $1.4 Billion." India eNews. 23 May 2008. http://www.indiaenews.com/middle-east/20080523/120158.htm

"Saudi company to invest in $250 million construction project." Kuwait Times. 22 May 2008. http://www.kuwaittimes.net/read_news.php?newsid=NTc5MTU4MzU=

"Shaping Israel's Tourism Policy to Encourage Regional Cooperation: Policy recommendations." The Peres Center for Peace. 17 May 2006. http://www.peres-center.org/RegionalTourismPolicyPaperMay2006.pdf

"Press Release for the Hotel Survey." Annual Report 2003. Palestinian Central Bureau of Statistics (PCBS). 2003. http://www.pcbs.gov.ps/Default.aspx?tabID=1&lang=en

"Press Release for the Hotel Survey." Annual Report 2004. Palestinian Central Bureau of Statistics (PCBS). 2004. http://www.pcbs.gov.ps/Portals/_pcbs/PressRelease/hotele04.pdf

"Press Release for the Hotel survey." Fourth Quarter 2005. Palestinian Central Bureau of Statistics (PCBS). 2005. http://pcbs.gov.ps/Portals/_pcbs/PressRelease/HOTELE0405.pdf

Chapter 8: Costs to the International Community

1. Oil, Tariffs and You
"Oil Hits $100 barrel: Crude oil prices in 1970-2008." BBC World News, 2 January 2008. http://news.bbc.co.uk/2/hi/business/7501939.stm

"Weekly All Countries Spot Price FOB Weighted by Estimated Export Volume (Dollars per Barrel)." Energy Information Administration (EIA), 2008. http://tonto.eia.doe.gov/dnav/pet/hist/wtotworldw.htm

Rubin, Jeff & Benjamin Tal. "Will Soaring Transport Costs Reverse Globalization." Strategecon. CIBC World Markets. 27 May 2008. http://research.cibcwm.com/economic_public/download/smay08.pdf

Krauss, Clifford. "Driving Less, Americans Finally React to Sting of Gas Prices, A Study Says." New York Times, 19 June 2008. http://www.nytimes.com/2008/06/19/business/19gas.html?_r=1&ref=business&oref=slogin

Murray, Lisa "Malaysian's Turn Out in Thousands to Defy Police." The Age, 7 July 2008. http://www.theage.com.au/world/malaysians-turn-out-in-thousands-to-defy-police-20080706-32mu.html

"Editorial: SBY Still Doesn't Get it." The Jakarta Post, 12 September 2008. http://www.thejakartapost.com/news/2008/07/07/editorial-sby-still-doesn039t-get-it.html

"More Airlines Fold as Fuel Prices Soar: IATA." AFP, 8 July 2008. http://news.asiaone.com/News/Latest+News/Business/Story/A1Story20080708-75407.html

"Oil Hits New High on Iran Fears." BBC World News, 11 July 2008. http://news.bbc.co.uk/2/hi/business/7501939.stm

Bourguinon Francois, Dalia Marin et al, Making Sense of Globalisation: A Guide to the Economic Issues, Centre for Economic Policy Research, 2002

2. No Fly List
"TSA Watchlist: December 2002." TSIS Transportation Security Intelligence Service. American Civil Liberties Union (ACLU), December 2002. http://www.aclunc.org/cases/landmark_cases/asset_upload_file371_3549.pdf

Kroft, Steve. "Unlikely Terrorists on No Fly List." Broadcast on 8 October 2006. CBS News, 10 June 2007. http://www.cbsnews.com/stories/2006/10/05/60minutes/main2066624.shtml

"'No Fly List' Could Blacklist Innocents." CTV.ca, 17 June 2007. http://www.ctv.ca/servlet/ArticleNews/story/CTVNews/20070617/nofly_list_070617/20070617?hub=TopStories

"Dr. Gunaratna: Core Al Qaeda Strength is Under 500." Agentura, 2008. http://www.agentura.ru/english/experts/gunaratna

"Al Qaeda." South Asian Terrorism Portal, 2001. http://www.satp.org/satporgtp/usa/Al_Queda.htm

Elliot, Michael. "Hate Club: Al Qaeda's web of terror." Time, 4 November 2001. http://www.time.com/time/nation/article/0,8599,182746,00.html

Bonner, Raymond. "A Nation Challenged: Terrors outposts, "Sleeper Cells' in Singapore show Al Qaeda's long reach." New York Times, 26 January 2002. http://query.nytimes.com/gst/fullpage.html?res=9F02E0DF143AF935A15752C0A9649C8B63

Gaubatz, Dave. "Sleeper Cells in the United States and Canada." American Thinker, 2 February 2007. http://www.americanthinker.com/2007/02/sleeper_cells_in_the_united_st.html

"Al Qaeda, Sleeper Cells." Global Security.org http://www.globalsecurity.org/military/world/para/al-qaida-sleeper-cells.htm

Feiser, Jonathan. "Evolution of the Al Qaeda Brand Name." Asian Times Online, 13 August 2004. http://www.atimes.com/atimes/Middle_East/FH13Ak05.html

American Civil Liberties Union (www.aclu.org) 2008.

"Air Travel Restrictions and Rules." Interview with Niccolo Melendex. Videojug, September 2006. www.videojug.com/interview/air-travel-security-restrictions-and-rules

Left, Sarah. "Human Rights Side-Lined Since September 11th." Guardian, 28 May 2002. http://www.guardian.co.uk/world/2002/may/28/humanrights.politics

3. Bill of War on Terror
"Funding the Global War on Terrorism." Yearbook 2008. pg. 183-184, Stockholm International Peace Research Institute (SIPRI), 2008.

"Economic Impact" Yearbook 2007. pg. 282, Stockholm International Peace Research Institute (SIPRI), 2008.

4. UN Bill for Peace-keeping
"Facts and Figures: Middle East: Peacekeeping." United Nations Website, 2008. http://www.un.org/Depts/dpko/dpko/currentops.shtml#mideast

5. EU Bills for the Palestinians
"How the European Commission is Responding to the Needs of the Palestinians." European Union @ United Nations Partnership in Action, March 2008. http://www.europa-eu-un.org/articles/en/article_7624_en.htm

"EU-Palestinian Authority Relations: EC Support for the Palestinians 2000-2006." European Union, 2000-2006 http://ec.europa.eu/external_relations/palestinian_authority/index_en.htm

6. Spread of Al Qaeda
"Timeline: Al Qaeda's Global Context." Frontline, PBS.org, 200-2001. http://www.pbs.org/wgbh/pages/frontline/shows/knew/etc/cron.html

"Eight Arrested in Paris for Deadly Tunisian Synagogue Bombing." CBC News, 5 November 2002. http://www.cbc.ca/story/world/national/2002/11/05/france_arrests021105.html

"Saudi Official Blames Al Qaeda for Riyadh Bombing." People Daily, 9 November 2003. http://english.peopledaily.com.cn/200311/09/eng20031109_127923.shtml

"Al Qaeda Car bombing and SAM Attack." Global Security.org, 2007. http://www.globalsecurity.org/security/profiles/al-qaeda_car_bombing_and_sam_attack.htm

"Istanbul Rocked by Double Bombing." BBC World News, 20 November 2003. http://news.bbc.co.uk/1/hi/world/europe/3222608.stm

"Madrid Bombing Trials: Key defendant refuses to testify." CNN. 15 February 2007. http://edition.cnn.com/2007/WORLD/europe/02/14/spain.trial.index.html

"London Attackers Meant to Kill." BBC World News, 22 July 2005. http://news.bbc.co.uk/1/hi/uk/4705117.stm

"Sharm El Sheikh Attacks Threaten Egypt's Recovery." AME info, 26 July 2005. http://www.ameinfo.com/64877.html

"Hotels Blast Kills Dozens in Jordan: Al Zarqawi prime suspect in nearly simultaneous suicide attacks." CNN, 10 November 2005. http://edition.cnn.com/2005/WORLD/meast/11/09/jordan.blasts/index.html

Bennhold, Katherine and Craig Smith. "Twin Bombs Kill Dozens in Algiers." New York Times, 12 December 2007. http://www.nytimes.com/2007/12/12/world/africa/12algiers.html

"Deaths per day, per year for Suicide Attacks and Vehicle Bombs." Iraq Body Count, 2003-2008. http://www.iraqbodycount.org/database/

7. The Return of the Taliban
"Afghanistan Study Group Report." Centre for the Study of the Presidency, January 2008. http://www.thepresidency.org/pubs/Afghan_Study_Group_final.pdf

"The Real Surge in 2007: Non-Combatant Deaths in Iraq and Afghanistan." Carnegie Council, January 2008. http://www.cceia.org/resources/articles_papers_reports/0003.html

"Coalition Military Fatalities by Year, Operation Enduring Freedom." iCasualties.org, September 2008. http://icasualties.org/oef/

"Suicide Attacks in Afghanistan, 2001-2007." United Nations Assistance Mission to Afghanistan, September 2007. http://www.unama-afg.org/docs/_UN-Docs/UNAMA%20-%20SUICIDE%20ATTACKS%20STUDY%20-%20

SEPT%209th%202007.pdf

Hamim, Javed. "2007 Ends with 137 Attacks in Afghanistan." Pajhwak Afghan News Agency, 1 Jauary 2008. http://www.afgha.com/?q=node/5510

"Iraq Proposes Time Table for 2010 US Withdrawal." The Dawn, 8 August 2008. http://www.dawn.com/2008/08/09/int1.htm

"Afghanistan Opium Survey 2008: Executive Summary." United Nations Office on Drugs and Crimes (UNODC), August 2008. http://www.unodc.org/documents/data-and-analysis/ExSum25August-standard.pdf

"Opium Cultivation in Afghanistan Down by a Fifth." United Nations Office on Drugs and Crimes (UNODC), 26 August 2008. http://www.unodc.org/unodc/en/frontpage/opium-cultivation-in-afghanistan-down-by-a-fifth.html

8. Ascent of Ayatollahs
"Final Distribution of PLC Seats, 2006 & 1996 elections." Central Elections Commission-Palestine. http://www.elections.ps/template.aspx?id=52

Ridolfo, Kathleen. "Iraq: Election Commission Releases Final Vote Results." Global Security.org, 20 January 2006. http://www.globalsecurity.org/wmd/library/news/iraq/2006/01/iraq-060120-rferl02.htm

Visser, Reider. "Beyond SCIRI and Abd Al Aziz al Hakim: The Silent Forces of the United Iraqi Alliance." Historiae, 20 January 2006. http://historiae.org/UIA.asp

Ratzlav-Katz, Nissan. "DM Barack in DC Warns of Iranian Influence." Israel National News, 29 July 2008. http://www.israelnationalnews.com/News/News.aspx/126991

Sieff, Martin. "Iran's Influence Growing in Iraq" United Press Internation (UPI), 12 October 2005. http://www.spacewar.com/news/iraq-05zzzzd.html

9. Loss of American Credibility
Telhami, Shibley. "Annual Arab Public Opinion Poll" Anwar Sadar Chair for Peace and Development, University of Maryland, March 2008. http://sadat.umd.edu/surveys/2008%20Arab%20Public%20Opinion%20Survey.ppt

"World View of US Role." BBC World Service Poll by GlobeScan, 2007. http://www.globescan.com/news_archives/bbcusop/

12. Closure of the Strait of Hormuz
Johnson, Toni. "Oil's trouble Spots." Council on Foreign Relations. 2 September 2008. http://www.washingtonpost.com/wp-dyn/content/article/2008/09/02/AR2008090201104.html

"Factbox-The Strait of Hormuz, Iran and the risk to oil." Global Security News. 27 March 2007. http://www.globalsecurity.org/org/news/2007/070327-hormuz-strait.htm

"Strait of Hormuz." The Robert Strauss Center, University of Texas. http://hormuz.robertstrausscenter.org/oil_market#_edn8

"Country Energy Data and Analysis." Energy Information Administration. http://www.eia.doe.gov/emeu/international/oilproduction.html

"Strait of Hormuz: Economic effects of disruption." Reuters. 25 April 2008. http://www.reuters.com/article/latestCrisis/idUSL25750348

"Global Oil Chokepoints." Global Equity Research, Lehman Brothers. 18 January 2008. http://www.deepgreencrystals.com/images/GlobalOilChokePoints.pdf

Chambers, Matt. "What Happens If Iran Blocks The Strait Of Hormuz." The Wall Street Journal. 27 August 2007. http://www.freerepublic.com/focus/f-news/1887549/posts

"OPEC Oil Export Revenues." Energy Information Administration. http://www.eia.doe.gov/emeu/cabs/OPEC_Revenues/Factsheet.html

"World Oil Outlook, 2007." Organization of the Petroleum Exporting Countries. 2007. http://www.opec.org/library/World%20Oil%20Outlook/pdf/WorldOilOutlook.pdf

ANNEXURE 1

INTERNATIONAL WORKSHOP ON COST OF CONFLICT IN THE MIDDLE EAST

Antalya, Turkey, 15-16 March 2008

Workshop Programme

March 15

Morning and afternoon:	Arrival of participants
19.30 onwards	**Welcome dinner for participants**

Welcome by
- Mr. Mevlut Çavuşoğlu, MP, Antalya, Turkey
- Mr. Sundeep Waslekar, President, Strategic Foresight Group
- Mr. Egemen Bağış, Vice Chairman of AK Party in charge of Foreign Affairs, MP, Istanbul, Turkey

Keynote Addresses by
- Ambassador Hesham Youssef, Chef de Cabinet for Secretary General, League of Arab States
- Prof. Dr. Mehmet Aydın, Minister of State, Turkey

March 16

9.00 - 10.00

Introductory Session

(Chaired and introduced by Mr. Yasar Yakis, MP, former Foreign Minister of Turkey, Head of the EU-Turkey Harmonisation Committee of Turkish Parliament, Turkey)
- Overview: Mr. Sundeep Waslekar, President of Strategic Foresight Group
- Keynote Address: Amb. Thomas Greminger, Head of Political Affairs, Human Security, in Federal Ministry of Foreign Affairs of Switzerland

10.00-11.00

Turkish Perspectives of the Cost

(Chaired and introduced by Mr. Egemen Bagis, MP, AK Parti Vice Chairman in Charge of Foreign Affairs, Turkey)
- Ms. Esra Cuhadar Gurkaynak, Assistant Professor at Political Science Department of Bilkent University, Turkey
- Mr. Kerem Kıratlı, Head of Department of Middle East of the Ministry of Foreign Affairs of the Republic of Turkey

11.00-11.30

Coffee Break

11.30-13.00

Social and Political Costs

(Chaired and introduced by Mr. Vidar Helgesen, former Deputy Minister of Foreign Affairs of Norway and Secretary General of International IDEA)
- Dr. Jon Pedersen, Managing Director, FAFO, Norway
- Amb. Abdel Raouf El Reedy, President, Egyptian Council for Foreign Affairs, Egypt
- Dr. Mahmoud Labadi, former Director of Aid Coordination and UN Specialized Agencies and former Director General of the Palestinian Legislative Council, Palestine

13.00-14.00	**Lunch**

14.00-16.00 **Economic Costs**

(Chaired and introduced by Dr. Mohammad Shtayyeh, President of PECDAR and former Minister of Housing and Public Works, Palestine)
- Prof Talaat Abdel Malek, Professor of Economics, American University of Cairo, Economic Advisor to the Government, Egypt
- Major General MK Shiyyab, Head of Cooperating Monitoring Centre, Jordan
- Dr. Riad Al Khouri, Director, Middle East Business Association, Jordan
- Dr. Haila Al Mekaimi, Head of Euro-Gulf Research Unit, Kuwait University, Kuwait

16.00-16.30 **Coffee Break**

16.30- 17.30 **Military Costs**

(Chaired and introduced by Brig. Gen. Dov Sedaqa, former Head of Civil Administration of the West Bank and currently with Economic Cooperation Foundation, Israel)
- Prof Efraim Inbar, Director, Begin Sadat Centre for Strategic Studies, Israel
- Dr. Mahdi Abdel Hadi, Chairman, Palestinian Academic Society for the Study of International Affairs

17.30-18.30 **Diplomatic and other costs**

(Chaired by Dr. Ephraim Sneh, former Minister for Health of Israel)
Amb Aly Maher, Director, Institute for Peace Studies, Bibliotheca Alexandrina, Egypt
- Mr. Salman Shaikh, Director for Policy, Office of Her Highness Sheikha Mozah, Qatar
- Mr. Niccolo Rinaldi, Deputy Secretary General, ALDE, European Parliament

18.30-19.00 **Concluding Session**

(Chaired by Mr. Saban Disli, MP, AK Parti Vice Chairman for Economic Affairs, Turkey)
- Ms. Ilmas Futehally, Strategic Foresight Group
- Concluding Remarks by Mr. Thomas Oertle, Swiss Federal Department of Foreign Affairs
Discussion on sources, inputs and suggestions for future research and workshops, including guidelines for aspects of costs not covered by the synopsis, cost escalation scenarios and cost reduction scenarios

19.30 **Formal dinner**

Hosted by Mr. Menderes Turel, Mayor of Antalya Metropolitan Municipality
Venue: ClubARMA, Antalya Castle

List of Participants

1. Amb. Abdel Raouf El Reedy, President, Egyptian Council for Foreign Affairs, Egypt

2. Prof Dr. Ali Çarkoğlu, Professor in Faculty of Art and Social Sciences of Sabancı University

3. Amb Aly Maher, Director, Institute for Peace Studies, Bibliotheca Alexandrina, Egypt

4. Mr. Cengiz Çandar, Journalist-Author, Turkey

5. Brig. Gen. Dov Sedaqa, former Head of Civil Administration of the West Bank and currently with Economic Cooperation Foundation, Israel

6. Mr. Egemen Bagis, MP, AK Parti Vice Chairman for Foreign Affairs, Turkey

7. Prof Efraim Inbar, Director, Begin Sadat Centre for Strategic Studies, Israel

8. Dr. Ephraim Sneh, former Minister of Health, Transportation and Defence, Israel

9. Ms. Esra Cuhadar Gurkaynak, Assistant Professor in Political Science Department of Bilkent University, Turkey

10. Dr. Haila Al Mekaimi, Head of Euro-Gulf Research Unit, Kuwait University, Kuwait

11. Amb Hesham Youssef, Chef de Cabinet for Secretary General, League of Arab States

12. Ms. Ilmas Futehally, Executive Director, Strategic Foresight Group, India

13. Dr. Jon Pedersen, Managing Director, FAFO, Norway

14. Prof Dr. Kemal Kirişçi, Professor at Political Science and International Relations Department of Bogazici University

15. Mr. Kerem Kıratlı, Head of Department of the Middle East of the Ministry of Foreign Affairs of the Republic of Turkey

16. Mr. Mahdi Abdel Hadi, Secretary General, Palestinian Academic Society for the Study of International Affairs, Palestine

17. Dr. Mahmoud Labadi, Director of Aid Coordination and UN Specialized Agencies and former Director General of the Palestinian Legislative Council, Palestine

18. Major General MK Shiyyab, Head of Cooperating Monitoring Centre, Jordan

19. Dr. Mohammad Shtayyeh, President of PECDAR, and former Minister of Housing and Public Works, Palestine

20. Prof Dr. Mehmet Aydın, Minister of State, Turkey

21. Mr. Mevlüt Çavuşoğlu, MP, Chairman for Turkish Delegation for Council of Europe, Turkey

22. Mr. Mustafa Akyol, Op-ed Author, Turkey

23. Mr. Niccolo Rinaldi, Deputy Secretary General, ALDE, European Parliament

24. Doç. Dr. Nuray Mert, Associate Professor and Faculty of Economy and Administration of İstanbul University

25. Dr. Riad Al Khouri, Director, Middle East Business Association, Jordan

26. Mr. Saban Disli, MP, AK Parti, Vice Chairman for Economic Affairs, Turkey

27. Mr. Salman Shaikh, Director for Research and Policy, Office of Her Highness Sheikha Mozah, Qatar

28. Mr. Sundeep Waslekar, President, Strategic Foresight Group, India

29. Dr. Taha Ozhan, Foundation for Political, Economic and Social Research, SETA, Turkey

30. Prof Talaat Abdel Malek, Professor of Economics, American University of Cairo, Economic Advisor to the Government, Egypt

31. Amb Thomas Greminger, Head of Political Division IV-Human Security, Federal Department of Foreign Affairs, Switzerland

32. Mr. Thomas Oertle, Head of the Middle East Desk at Federal Department of Foreign Affairs, Switzerland

33. Mr. Vidar Helgesen, former Deputy Minister for Foreign Affairs, Secretary General of International IDEA, Sweden

34. Mr. Yasar Yakis, MP, former Foreign Minister, Head of EU-Turkey Harmonisation Committee of Turkish Parliament, Turkey

35. Mr. Yusuf Ziya Irbec, MP representing Antalya, Turkey

36. Ms. Camino Kavanagh, Special Adviser, International IDEA, Sweden

Conference Coordinators

• Ms. Devika Mistry, Research Analyst, Strategic Foresight Group, India

• Ms. Ayse Sozen, Department of Foreign Affairs, AK Party, Turkey

SECOND INTERNATIONAL WORKSHOP ON COST OF CONFLICT IN THE MIDDLE EAST

Zurich, Switzerland, August 18-19, 2008

Workshop Programme

August 18

18:30-19:30	**Informal Reception**
19:30-19:45	**From A to Z (Antalya to Zurich): Remarks by Mr. Egemen Bagis**
19:45-20:15	**Introduction by participants**
20:15-20:45	**Keynote Address by Ambassador Thomas Greminger**
20:45-22.15	**Dinner**

August 19

09:00-09:30	**Introduction to Scenario-building Process and Key Questions** Chaired by Dr. Ephraim Sneh - Introduction to Scenario-Building Process by Mr. Sundeep Waslekar - Remarks by Dr. Ephraim Sneh on Key Questions about Future Risks of Cost Escalation and Opportunities for Cooperation between Israel and the Arab region
09:30-11:00	**Drivers of Costs of Conflict and Cost of Peace-building** Chaired by Ambassador Hesham Youssef
11:00-11:30	**Coffee Break**
11:30-13:00	**Conflict Escalation Ladder** Chaired by Mr. Vidar Helgesen
13:00-14:00	**Lunch Break**
14:00-15:30	**Peace Building Ladder** Chaired by Mr. Tony Klug
15:30-16:00	**Coffee Break**
16:00-17:30	**Wild Cards** Chaired by Mr. Salman Shaikh
17:30-18:30	**Concluding Observations** Chaired by Mr. Jean-Daniel Ruch, Ambassador at Large for Special Assignments, Federal Department of Foreign Affairs of Switzerland - "Generating public policy impact of the Cost of Conflict Study", views of participants - Comments by Ms. Ilmas Futehally, Executive Director of Strategic Foresight Group - Concluding Address by the Chair
19:30-22.30	**Informal Networking Dinner** hosted by Federal Department of Foreign Affairs of the Government of Switzerland

List of Participants

1. Ambassador Hesham Youssef, Chef de Cabinet, Arab League Secretary General's Office, Egypt

2. Mr. Salman Shaikh, Director for Research and Policy, Office of Her Highness Sheikha Mozah, Qatar

3. Prof. Yair Hirschfeld, Director General, Economic Cooperation Foundation, Israel

4. Prof. Kamal Field Al Basri, Chairman, Institute for Economic Reform, Iraq

5. Mr. Egemen Bagis, MP, Vice Chairman for Foreign Affairs, AK Parti, Turkey

6. Ms. Ica Wahbeh, Managing Editor, Jordan Times, Jordan

7. Prof. Azza El Kholy, Advisor, Institute for Peace Studies at Bibliotheca Alexandrina, Egypt

8. Dr. Esra Cuhadar Gurkaynak, Assistant Professor in Political Science Department of Bilkent University, Turkey

9. Dr. Mahmoud Labadi, former Director of Aid Coordination and former Director General of the Palestinian Legislative Council, Palestine

10. Ms. Bambi Sheleg, Editor in Chief of Eretz Aheretz, Israel

11. Dr. Riad Al Khouri, Director, Middle East Business Association, Jordan

12. Mr. Vidar Helgesen, former Deputy Minister for Foreign Affairs of Norway, Secretary General of International IDEA, Sweden

13. Mr. Yasar Yakis, MP, former Foreign Minister, Head of EU-Turkey Harmonisation Committee of the Turkish Parliament, Turkey

14. Prof. Khalil Gebara, Chief Executive, Transparency International National Office, Lebanon

15. Ms. Eliane Metni, National Coordinator, Director International Education Association and Chair of iEARN, Lebanon

16. Ms. Nicole Nasseh, Representative, UNDP Peace-building Project, Lebanon

17. Dr. Darwish Ghaloum Al-Emadi, Director of Public Opinion Poll Center, Qatar University, Qatar

18. Dr. Saif Shaheen Al-Murikhi, Associate Professor, Humanities Dept., College of Arts and Sciences, Qatar University, Qatar

19. Dr. Sahar Al Qawasmi, Member, Palestinian Legislative Council, Palestine

20. Dr. Tony Klug, Vice Chairman of Arab-Jewish Forum and author of several booklets on the Middle East for the Fabian Society, UK

21. Dr. Mark Taylor, Director, FAFO, Norway

22. Dr. Mehran Kamrava, Director of Center for International and Regional Studies, Georgetown University, Qatar

23. Dr. Robert Muggah, Research Director, Small Arms. Survey, Switzerland

24. Ms. Camino Kavanogh, Special Adviser to the Secretary General of International IDEA, Sweden

25. Mr. Itamar Yaar, Former Deputy Head of the Israeli National Security Council, Israel

26. Dr. Ephraim Sneh, former Israeli Cabinet Minister and Chairman of the "Strong Israel" Party, Israel

27. Dr. Nimrod Novik, Senior Vice-President, Merhav Group of Companies, Israel

28. Mr. Sundeep Waslekar, President, Strategic Foresight Group, India

29. Ms. Ilmas Futehally, Executive Director, Strategic Foresight Group, India

30. Ms. Gitanjali Bakshi, Research Analyst, Strategic Foresight Group, India

31. Ambassador Thomas Greminger, Head of Political Division IV-Human Security, Federal Department of Foreign Affairs, Switzerland

32. Mr. Thomas Oertle, Head of the Middle East Desk, Federal Department of Foreign Affairs, Switzerland

33. Ms. Barbara Fontana, Office of Special Envoy for the Middle East, Switzerland

34. Mr. Jean-Daniel Ruch, Ambassador at Large for Special Assignments, Federal Department of Foreign Affairs, Switzerland

35. Ms. Bettina Schucan, Programme Officer, Office of the Ambassador at Large for Special Assignments, Federal Department of Foreign Affairs, Switzerland

36. Ms. Judith Schatzman, Office of Ambassador at Large for Special Assignments, Federal Department of Foreign Affairs, Switzerland

ACKNOWLEDGEMENTS

Cost of Conflict in the Middle East

In June 2007, The Rt. Hon. Lord Alderdice convened a meeting of senior European leaders, representatives of important institutions from the Middle East, and other experts at the House of Lords. It was supported by Friedrich Naumann Stiftung of Germany. At this meeting, Ambassador Hesham Youssef, Head of Secretary General's Office in the League of Arab States and Richard Kerr, a former high ranking member of the federal administration in the United States, recommended that Strategic Foresight Group should undertake a study of the cost of conflict in the Middle East, drawing from its experience in preparing similar studies for the India-Pakistan and Sri Lanka conflicts. This is how the idea for this study was born.

Honourable Recep Tayyip Erdogan, Prime Minister of Turkey, welcomed this idea in a meeting with Strategic Foresight Group on the margins of the first Alliance of Civilizations Forum in Madrid and offered to host a workshop of regional experts at Antalya in Turkey. The Swiss Government hosted the second international workshop for experts from the Middle East in Zurich to enable Strategic Foresight Group to test its research in progress and build scenarios for peace and conflict in the region.

Ambassador Thomas Greminger, Head of Political Affairs Division IV in the Swiss Federal Department of Foreign Affairs; Vidar Helgesen, former Deputy Foreign Minister of Norway; Egemen Bagis, Deputy Chairman of AK Party and Member of Parliament for Istanbul; Ambassador Hesham Youssef of the Arab League; and Salman Shaikh, Head of Policy and Research in the Office of Her Highness of Qatar formed the Core Group to provide diplomatic, intellectual and practical support for the project. Dr. Abdulla Al-Kubaisi, Executive Director of the Office of Her Highness of Qatar, also extended his support.

More than fifty experts including former ministers, heads of research institutes, and analysts from almost all countries affected by conflicts in the Middle East participated in the two workshops, provided research input in the form of short papers, advised the research team, and made valuable data available to them. Their names and titles are mentioned on the credit page and in the annexures. The Core Group, as well as Prof Yair Hirschfeld of Israel and Ambassador Jean-Daniel Ruch of Switzerland reviewed the previous drafts of this report. Prof Yair Hirschfeld, Ephraim Sneh and Mahmoud Labadi facilitated several meetings for the SFG team during their visit to Israel and Palestine Territories.

Strategic Foresight Group acknowledges the involvement and support of these individuals and institutions with a deep sense of gratitude. In particular, SFG most profusely thanks the sponsors: AK Party of Turkey, Federal Department of Foreign Affairs of Switzerland, Ministry of Foreign Affairs of Norway and the Qatar Foundation. However, Strategic Foresight Group takes the sole responsibility for the final output of the project and any errors or omissions that may be unknowingly associated with it.